PEOPLE PERSON

HOW TO TALK TO ANYONE, IMPROVE SOCIAL
AWKWARDNESS, AND COMMUNICATE WITH EASE
AND CONFIDENCE

SANDY R. WILLIAMS

CONTENTS

Introduction   7

1. LET'S TALK FIRST ABOUT WHY
YOU'RE STRUGGLING   11
Consequences   12
Why You're Having a Hard Time   16
Human Communication and the Brain   19
What is Social Awkwardness?   24
What Does Science Say About Social
Anxiety?   28
Introversion Explained by Science   30
Shyness Uncovered   33
Communication is a Skill   35
Summary Box   36

2. OVERCOMING NEGATIVITY   37
Negative Thinking Affects Social Skills   38
Overcoming Negative Thought Patterns   41
We Are Hardwired for Negativity   47
Practicing Self-Compassion   54
Exercise: Stopping Negative Thinking   58
Action Steps   59

3. GETTING OUT OF YOUR SHELL   61
Self-Esteem and Communication   62
Building Self-Confidence   67
Becoming a Confident Communicator   73
Confidence Exercises   77
Action Steps   81

4. EVERYONE IS ALWAYS
   COMMUNICATING—EVEN WITHOUT
   WORDS   83
   Nonverbal Communication   84
   Types of Nonverbal Communication   90
   Emotional Awareness   97
   How to Read People   99
   Action Steps   103

5. LISTENING TO UNDERSTAND   107
   Active Listening   108
   Active Listening Cues   110
   How to Actively Listen   114
   Examples of Active Listening in
   Conversations   119
   Action Steps   123

6. HOW DO YOU ASK THE RIGHT
   QUESTIONS?   125
   The Importance of Asking Questions In
   Conversations–Beyond The Obvious   126
   Question Formulation   129
   Question Quality   137
   The Role of Language   143
   Action Steps   149

7. HANDLING HARD-TO-HANDLE
   PEOPLE   151
   What Makes Someone a Difficult Person?   152
   Handling Difficult People   155
   Communicating With Difficult People   158
   Overcoming Communicating Hurdles
   with Difficult People   163
   More Communication Tips   165
   Action Steps   167

8. PRACTICING SMALL TALK AND
   BEING GOOD AT IT   169
   Mastering the Art of Small Talk   170
   Small Talk Topics   175
   Action Steps   185

   Conclusion   189
   References   191

INTRODUCTION

> *The way we communicate with others and with ourselves ultimately determines the quality of our lives.*

— TONY ROBBINS

Have you ever been in a situation when you had absolutely no idea what to say to someone?

Maybe you were on a train next to a person you'd spoken to before, but you were with a group of friends. But now, with just the two of you, you have no clue how to start a conversation or even keep one going. Or maybe you started a new job, and while you may have nailed the interview, day-to-day small talk with your boss and coworkers was strained and awkward?

Sometimes, despite your best intentions, you end up worrying so much about saying or doing the wrong thing that you end up saying nothing at all. Or you overthink situations and conjure up outrageous scenarios in your mind, imagining all sorts of negative outcomes that never actually happen.

Overthinking is a frequent occurrence for many; however, for those who endure this regularly, it can be a hindrance that's both physically and mentally draining. Thankfully, you can find comfort in knowing that you're not alone.

According to the book *Awkward: The Science of Why We're Socially Awkward and Why That's Awesome* by Ty Tashiro, approximately 15% of people have social skill challenges and communication problems that are thought to manifest as social awkwardness. Social anxiety has a significant role in the development of social awkwardness in many people and it goes beyond simply feeling shy. In fact, the National Institute of Mental Health reports that 12.1% of U.S. adults experience a social anxiety disorder (Social Anxiety Disorder, n.d.). Understanding social awkwardness and its impact is crucial to overcoming it. And in this book, you'll learn what it takes to do just that.

Each chapter is packed with extensive research and information to help you become a people person when you need or want to be. As someone who used to be extremely socially awkward, I know your challenges and frustrations. Breaking free from my shell has given me a deep understanding of what it takes. My goal is to use my expertise to help you break free too and guide you towards a better life with strategic techniques, essential tips, and advice.

By following this book from chapter to chapter, you'll have the tools needed for a seamless transformation into the person you aim to become. You'll be able to apply the book's key takeaways immediately and start practicing the art of talking to anyone. You'll learn how to reframe your thoughts, read body language, make small talk, build confidence, and form meaningful relationships.

So, sit back, relax, and enjoy *People Person*. Your future self will thank you for it.

1

LET'S TALK FIRST ABOUT WHY YOU'RE STRUGGLING

As individuals, our ability to communicate is an inherent trait we possess from birth. However, the path to successful interactions is not always straightforward. From the early stages of speech development in children, where unintelligible babbling gradually transforms into meaningful words and sentences, to the intricate landscape of adult communication, numerous factors shape our ability to connect with others.

The challenges we face in communication stem from a range of influences, including language disparities, diverse cultural backgrounds, unique personal experiences, and individual communication styles. These elements can give rise to obstacles, misunderstandings, and difficulties in effectively conveying our thoughts and ideas.

In this chapter, our focus will be on exploring the factors that may contribute to the challenges you may encounter when engaging with others. We will also delve into the profound impact that poor communication can have on various aspects of your life.

CONSEQUENCES

Did you know that poor communication skills can significantly affect your overall life satisfaction and feelings of loneliness? It's true! Research published in the Journal of Happiness Studies has shown that the frequency of face-to-face interaction and the number of close relationships you have are powerful predictors of life satisfaction and loneliness (Amati et al., 2018).

Interestingly, the study also found that certain types of interpersonal media, such as video chat and voice calls, were associated with greater life satisfaction. On the other hand, lean media, such as text messaging, were indirectly associated with greater loneliness through relationship maintenance frustration.

These findings highlight the importance of improving your communication skills in both your personal and professional relationships. But let's take a closer look at the various ways in which poor communication can affect your day-to-day experiences and relationships to fully understand the potential negative consequences.

Misunderstandings

Misunderstandings can be a real headache, especially when they happen because of poor communication. When you're not clear in your communication, it's easy for your colleagues and management to make assumptions about you and your abilities. This can lead to confusion, frustration, and sometimes failed expectations.

For example, let's say you're a project manager tasked with leading a team to complete a critical project. You're feeling the pressure, so you decide to communicate with your team via email instead of in-person meetings. However, your email is vague and lacks specific details, leaving your team unsure about their roles and responsibilities. This leads to missed deadlines, a poorly executed project, and ultimately, unhappy clients.

As a result, your team may lose faith in your leadership skills, and your relationship with them may become strained. And your management team may doubt your competence.

In your personal life, poor communication can also lead to misunderstandings and conflicts with friends, family, and loved ones. This could cause hurt feelings, damaged relationships, and even breakups or divorces.

Missed Opportunities

Missed opportunities are a bummer, especially when they happen because of poor communication. In the workplace, a lack of clear communication can lead to missed opportunities for growth and advancement, as decision-makers may not know how to support your development. For example, if you don't communicate your interest in a new project or your desire to take on more responsibility, you may miss out on opportunities to showcase your skills and abilities. The same holds true for personal relationships. If you don't communicate your feelings or needs to your partner, you may miss out on the chance to deepen your relationship and build a stronger emotional connection.

Needless Conflict

Who wants to spend their time dealing with unnecessary conflict, whether it's in their personal life or professional life? Imagine you're taking the lead in planning a vacation with your partner. Unbeknownst to you, you two have very different ideas about what makes a great vacation. You like to relax by the poolside, and they prefer to be on the go. Instead of discussing your preferences openly, you both assume that the other knows what you prefer. When you arrive at your destination, it becomes apparent that you have very different expectations, which leads to tension and conflict. A similar scenario could easily happen in a professional environment. Uncommunicated or poorly communicated desires and expectations can make any interaction contentious.

There's a Chance You'll Inspire Distrust

Poor communication may cause others to lose faith in you, especially if they believe you are evasive or that you withhold information. For instance, if you, as a manager, do not inform your team about a promotion opportunity, they may lose trust in you and look for jobs elsewhere.

You Might Not Get the Help or Resources You Require

As impressive as it would be, we can't read the minds of others and they can't read ours. This means that in order to advance and achieve our goals, we must rely on the power of communication. For instance, when facing difficulties at work, failing to inform your manager or being unable to clearly explain the problem can cause missed opportunities for valuable advice and resources. Over time, this can negatively affect your performance and hinder your professional development.

WHY YOU'RE HAVING A HARD TIME

Making connections with others involves building an emotional and social bond. These bonds are important because they make us feel like we truly belong.

If you're finding it difficult to connect with others, there could be a range of possible reasons why. Negative emotions like fear and doubt can often be the leading causes, and they may even cause mood swings that further hinder your ability to form meaningful connections. Sometimes feelings of isolation and distance may indicate a more serious issue that requires attention and support.

Recognizing the root causes that may contribute to social connection issues is crucial to the recovery process. Below, you will find a few additional reasons you might be having a hard time.

Social and Communication Skills Are Lacking

The inability to connect with people may be related to a lack of social or communication skills.

Suppose the idea of having a casual chat with someone makes you uneasy. It could be harder to get over the awkward initial few months of a relationship and develop a deeper connection.

There are more factors that might affect communication. For instance, poor social skills might result from low self-esteem or lack of confidence. It could be beneficial, under these circumstances, to speak with a mental health expert.

Negativity

If you tend to focus on the negative aspects of your relationships with others, you may find yourself feeling disconnected and isolated. This can result from a variety of factors, such as holding others to unreasonably high standards or a lack of empathy.

Difficulty or the inability to understand the emotions of others will inevitably make it harder to connect with them. Without empathy, it's difficult to relate to others and to appreciate their perspectives and experiences.

Mental Health Problems

Navigating the challenges of communication and connection during times of mental health struggles presents a complex and delicate situation. Individuals grappling with depression, for instance, often encounter feelings of hopelessness, diminished motivation, and a general disinterest in social engagement. As a result, they may find themselves retreating from relationships and seeking solitude, which poses obstacles in establishing and sustaining significant bonds.

Trauma

The impact of trauma on interpersonal connections cannot be overlooked. Those who have experienced trauma, especially during their formative years, may find it challenging to trust others.

Instances of abuse, betrayal, or bullying, for instance, can significantly hinder one's ability to place trust in new individuals in social settings. Moreover, traumatic experiences can give rise to additional psychological issues that can further disrupt the establishment of meaningful connections later in life.

Extreme Use of Social Media

The widespread use of technology, social media, and remote work has provided us with constant digital contact. However, excessive internet usage may have adverse effects on our capacity to establish meaningful connections.

Traditionally, people connect through shared interests, activities, or aspirations. While the internet and social media platforms can aid in fostering such connections to some extent, studies suggest that spending excessive time online may, in fact, hinder the development of authentic and impactful relationships (Lomanowska & Guitton, 2016).

HUMAN COMMUNICATION AND THE BRAIN

How we communicate with certain people depends on how we perceive them and the environment. Let's say a stranger pulls up in their vehicle beside you and asks for directions. There are several factors that will determine how you respond to them or if you'll welcome their inquiry. Factors like the type of vehicle they're driving, their estimated age, their mannerisms, or if you hear a foreign accent, may all play a role in how you respond. You may decide to speak slower, use basic words, or include hand gestures.

As humans, we effortlessly adapt our communication style to match the person we're speaking to. However, doing it so rapidly still holds an element of intrigue. A recent study shows that a specific region of the brain known as the prefrontal cortex plays a vital role in refining our communication based on the person we're interacting with (Stolk, 2017).

People who have experienced impairment in the prefrontal cortex area of their brains possess the ability to communicate, but they encounter difficulties in adjusting their communication style to accommodate the abilities of the people they're speaking to. This sets them apart from those without brain damage and those with brain damage in other regions.

Therefore, the prefrontal cortex plays a vital role in how we communicate. In the upcoming sections, we will explore supporting evidence that reinforces this claim.

The Phineas Gage Story

Phineas Gage was a railroad construction worker back in the 1800s. He was the survivor of a horrific work-related accident that involved an inch-thick iron rod impaling his left cheek and tearing through his brain before exiting his skull. Despite the force and impact of the rod, he quickly regained consciousness and was astonishingly still able to speak and move. It was later learned that the rod damaged the prefrontal portion of his brain.

This horrific event raised a multitude of questions like, how important is the prefrontal cortex in our day-to-day lives? And what other functions does it have that are yet to be unearthed?

Although Phineas didn't succumb to his injuries, some people who knew him confirmed they noticed significant changes to his mental abilities, as well as behavioral changes which made him noticeably different from the person he was before.

His case set early neurology on an unprecedented path and paved the way for new perspectives of the functionalities of the brain, how the different parts interacted with one another, and how this affected an individual's overall personality and behavior. One of the first key findings suggested the frontal lobe's involvement in shaping personality.

Today, there's a deeper understanding of how the frontal cortex assists with higher functions such as reasoning, social cognition, and language. The evolution and improvement of neuroscience, the study of the functions and operations of the brain, has provided newfound information regarding the impact and necessity of the prefrontal cortex in everyday life.

To give you a visual description of what this part of the brain looks like in action, picture yourself having a conversation with a stranger. Would you immediately share intimate information about yourself? For those without prefrontal cortex damage, the answer is no. However, studies have revealed that individuals with acute prefrontal cortex damage have little to no control over recognizing when sharing personal information is appropriate and when it is not. This means they openly share private details about their lives, even if they experience feelings of regret afterwards (Stolk, 2017).

This showed the importance of the prefrontal cortex during social interactions. The effectiveness of our interactions with others relies heavily on the functionality of this specific region of the brain.

Studying Communication With the Help of a Computer Game

Researchers conducted an experiment using a computer game where players communicated anonymously through avatars. The goal of the experiment was to show that individuals with intact prefrontal cortex adjusted their tone, pace, and word choice based on their assumptions about their partner's age and intellectual level.

The goal of the game was for one player to guide their partner to an acorn on the game board using only verbal commands. The participants were told they would play with two different partners, a child, and an adult, but in reality, they were interacting with researchers.

The study found that individuals with prefrontal brain damage failed to adjust their communication according to the person they were communicating with, unlike healthy individuals and patients with brain damage elsewhere (Stolk, 2017).

Difference in Communication

The results of the experiment strongly supported the hypothesis that individuals with prefrontal brain damage struggle to adjust their communication style appropriately. This finding contradicts previous beliefs that suggested a lack of willingness or capacity to communicate with such patients.

Simply put, patients with prefrontal brain damage can still communicate effectively, but their ability to adapt their communication to suit their listener is significantly impaired.

WHAT IS SOCIAL AWKWARDNESS?

Stepping into the world of social awkwardness provides a profound understanding of why individuals may feel overwhelmed by social interactions or struggle with communication in social settings.

Though it's true that human beings are social creatures by nature, not everyone has an innate ability to effortlessly bond with others. While we try to encourage this in children from a young age, whether at school or play, some individuals still grow up to experience social awkwardness.

It's important to note that feeling a bit uneasy during a social interaction does not automatically classify someone as socially awkward. Therefore, it becomes essential to delve into the true nature of social awkwardness and distinguish it from other commonly misunderstood conditions.

What Is It?

Social awkwardness arises when we find ourselves in a particular situation that triggers our fear of not being accepted. It's an overwhelming feeling of distress and discomfort. People grappling with social awkwardness often stress about saying the wrong thing and overthink what's expected of them in social settings. As a result, they tend to turn inward and become hyper-focused on self-monitoring.

Comparing Social Anxiety to Social Awkwardness

Although social awkwardness is accompanied by intense emotions and often leads to physiological changes, it differs significantly from social anxiety. Social anxiety is a recognized medical condition, social anxiety disorder (SAD), that can hinder one's social functioning and involves experiencing intense and recurring emotional distress in social situations.

Those with SAD may fear common social interactions, being teased or criticized, being watched, and interpersonal relationships, often leading to avoidance. When confronted with such circumstances, suffers of SAD may experience:

- difficulty swallowing
- increased heart rate
- increased perspiration
- trembling

While individuals who experience social awkwardness may or may not address their situation, those with SAD typically require treatment to manage their condition.

Comparing Introversion to Social Awkwardness

Although introversion and social awkwardness may appear similar at first glance, they are different. Introverts draw energy from solitude, introspection, and reflection, while extroverts gain energy from social interactions and companionship. This makes introversion more of a personality trait than a disorder. It is important to note that just because someone is introverted and prefers to reflect internally before making decisions; it does not mean they are incapable of interacting with others comfortably.

The key difference between introversion and social awkwardness is that introverts may prefer smaller groups or solitude, but they do not necessarily find social interactions unbearable. In contrast, socially awkward individuals may feel highly uncomfortable in social situations and may not know the social norms and rules that govern social interactions. It is important to recognize these differences and not conflate the two, as this can lead to misunderstandings and misinterpretations of behavior.

Comparing Autism to Social Awkwardness

Autism has often been mistaken for social awkwardness, probably because of how uncomfortable individuals with either condition appear in social settings. Autistic individuals, however, may not feel awkward but appear awkward as they sometimes lack the understanding needed to navigate and follow social norms. Additionally, they might fixate on particular themes only, which often leads people to think the person is unwilling to try new things.

While some of these tendencies can be true for socially awkward people, autism can't be compared to it. It is a complex condition and manifests in an assortment of ways. The impact it has on the individual's life is far greater than mere social awkwardness.

Aside from their lack of social skills, many autistic individuals also suffer from cognitive impairments, which makes tasks like eating, bathing, or dressing extremely difficult and exhausting. There are also those who experience hindrances in their capacity to learn because of this disorder.

In the past, it was believed that those with autism lacked the intellectual capacity to grasp the nuances of social interaction, as well as failed to experience empathy; however, King Online (2018) revealed how modern findings rebuffed this perception. It was further revealed that, just like every other individual, autistic people do, in fact, desire social connectedness and experience genuine emotion. Additionally, they also consider how their behavior and choices will affect those around them.

So, as much as social awkwardness is present in many autistic people, it doesn't mean a socially awkward person is autistic. Rather, socially awkward people are affected and triggered by their surroundings as opposed to the core functionality of their brain (as is with autism). It's also important to note that just because a person has autism, doesn't automatically mean they will be socially awkward.

WHAT DOES SCIENCE SAY ABOUT SOCIAL ANXIETY?

Research shows that social anxiety is more common than we think, with at least 5% of people suffering from it to some degree. That said, women are more likely to have it than men (Gill, 2021).

Still, many people don't understand what causes the symptoms of social anxiety, nor do they believe in the scientific support this condition has. Which is why we're going to dive deeper into this subject, to help provide insight into this misunderstood affliction.

The Amygdala

Research has shown that socially anxious individuals tend to have increased activity in the amygdala, the part of the brain that regulates emotions (Gill, 2021). When the brain activates the fear response, the body and brain go into a state of fight, flight, or freeze.

Fortunately, a skilled hypnotherapist can help stabilize the fight or flight response through effective communication with the amygdala and limbic system. This can induce relaxation and calmness, thus mitigating the fear response. Additionally, deep breathing and mindful meditation are exercises that can be done independently before social situations. Self-hypnosis is also an option worth considering.

Individuals who do not experience social discomfort or anxiety have a different type of amygdala response. This is because of the functions of the central part of the brain, which help us interpret and evaluate information received through our senses. As a result, these individuals can remain composed and rational, even in highly stimulating social situations.

INTROVERSION EXPLAINED BY SCIENCE

We've already learned introverts exhibit similar signs to that of social anxiety and social awkwardness, despite it being entirely different. But there is an intriguing scientific explanation why introverts struggle to express thoughts, particularly when feeling pressured, which might surprise you. Let's delve into the science behind this phenomenon.

Internal Information Processing

For introverts, trying to find the right word in a conversation can be a challenge. This is known as "word retrieval," and it can cause them to fall behind faster-talking extroverts in social situations, or to come across as unsure of themselves at work or in class. They may hesitate to speak up or raise their hand because they know it can be difficult to articulate their thoughts on the spot.

One reason word retrieval can be tricky for introverts is because they tend to process information deeply and mull over ideas and analyze them from different angles before speaking. When they're lost in thought, even about something as simple as what to have for breakfast, it can be hard to find the right words to express themselves. Unlike extroverts, introverts don't tend to think out loud or verbalize thoughts as much, prefer-ring to process thoughts quietly within themselves.

A Preference for Long-Term Memory

Long-term memory refers to memories that are stored in a part of the brain that makes it harder, sometimes impossible, to forget, but often outside of our conscious awareness. Some long-term memories are easily accessible, while others are harder to recall. Introverts favor long-term memory while extroverts favor working memory. Working memory is ideal for readily recalling information that only needs to be stored for a limited time. Because introverts prefer long-term memory, accessing working memories is often problematic.

Accessing long-term memories is a tedious task and often requires specific triggers to retrieve information; however, an introvert is quite skilled at doing so. You often see the mental wheels of an introvert turning as they become silent while attempting to access such archived information.

Further, if an introvert tells you how events unfolded many years ago on a particular occasion, nine times out of ten, you can take their word for it. This is because introverts make a concerted effort to store vital pieces of information that will trigger the entire event when stimulated.

Exacerbated by Anxiety

Another common misconception about introversion is that one is naturally timid and socially anxious.

Though it may be true that struggling to find the best words to express oneself in the moment may increase levels of anxiety, it doesn't mean introverts have social anxiety. When introverts are deeply engrossed in processing information and feel mentally drained from social interactions, anxiety has a way of sneaking in.

Here's the thing: anxiety takes a poll on mental energy and can even interfere with memory. During times of anxiety, the stress hormone cortisol floods the system, affecting the brain, leading to memory lapses and difficulties with recall.

Why Writing is Simpler?

Have you ever noticed that introverts often feel more comfortable expressing themselves through writing rather than in spoken conversations? They tend to gravitate towards emails and text messages over face-to-face meetings and phone calls. In fact, journaling has been hailed as a helpful practice for introverts, enabling them to delve into their thoughts and emotions with greater clarity.

But why do introverts have this preference for writing? It all comes down to how their brains are wired. You see, written words activate specific neural pathways that seem to flow more smoothly for introverts. It's like their thoughts effortlessly glide onto the paper or screen, allowing them to communicate with ease and express their thoughts and ideas.

SHYNESS UNCOVERED

Although shyness and social anxiety are different, the terms are frequently used interchangeably. People often feel uncomfortable in social situations because of shyness. Shyness doesn't always prevent someone from performing when necessary, but social anxiety, as we've learned, can be a more serious condition that negatively affects a person's overall well-being.

Though shyness isn't always a bad thing, some of its characteristics, such as passivity and reduced eye contact, could be mistaken for uncertainty, nervousness, or despondence. Even if some people have an inherent tendency toward timidness, feeling uncomfortable in strange situations is common.

Surely, you've witnessed the stark contrast between individuals who exude confidence and those who struggle through social situations. As we mature, some conquer shyness, blossoming into more extroverted and vocal people.

Traits of Shyness

Some common traits associated with shyness include:

- being reserved and quiet
- reluctance to try new things
- attempting to blend into the surroundings or go unnoticed
- neglecting eye contact
- overwhelming feelings of being out-of-place
- excessive fidgeting (playing with your fingers, clothing items, face, hair, etc.)

Signs That You're Shy

Shyness manifests physically in the following ways:

- elevated heart rate
- blushing
- lightheadedness

would you date yourself

- unusual feelings of nausea
- perspiring

knowing yourself as you do?

COMMUNICATION IS A SKILL

Communication, like so many aspects of our lives, is highly influenced by our socio-economic status and culture. Everyone has their own distinct manner of expression, and our perception of communication is also affected by our cultures and social development. There are certain values that play significant roles in how we view our own quality of communication and that of others, so it's imperative that we be mindful of the fact that communication style is crucial to our interactions.

You might be quick to assume that your communication style and methods are unflawed. However, take a moment to really think about what your traditions, customs, values, and personal insights suggest about the way you communicate.

Language is only one part of a person's communication style, which is probably why we often have misunderstandings while being completely oblivious to where the confusion lies. Perhaps it was your tone or a gesture you made that was misconstrued because it's common in one culture and unheard of in another.

These are all things to consider when trying to establish a neutral communication style that will present minimal misunderstandings.

SUMMARY BOX

Things to remember from this chapter:
- The consequences of being unable to communicate effectively includes having many misunderstanding, missing opportunities, being caught in conflicts, mistrust and low morale.
- There may be a lot of reasons you are having trouble communicating, such as past trauma, mental health issues, negativity and excessive social media.
- Social awkwardness, social anxiety, shyness and introvertness are different. However, they can all contribute to having a hard time communicating.
- Effective communication is a skill that is learned. However, a number of factors, including cultural influences can contribute to how we communicate.

In this chapter, we looked at how and why communication can be hard and some consequences of ineffective communication. In the following chapter, we will dive into overcoming negativity for effective communication.

2

OVERCOMING NEGATIVITY

Have you ever noticed how negative thoughts can creep into your mind, even when you don't want them to? It's like they come out of nowhere and take over. Negative thoughts make you feel bad about yourself or the situation you're in. Well, it turns out that negative thinking can actually affect your social skills, too.

A study from 2012 found that people who struggle with negative thoughts have more trouble communicating effectively (Serin et al., 2012). Negative thoughts can act as a barrier, preventing you from reaching your fullest potential.

There are ways, however, to overcome negative thinking, but we must first understand how it affects social skills and how to recognize it.

NEGATIVE THINKING AFFECTS SOCIAL SKILLS

The power of negative thinking extends its influence across multiple facets of our lives. Perhaps one of its most significant repercussions lies in its effect on our social interactions. Within the intricate web of our thoughts, negative patterns often breed self-doubt and reinforce detrimental beliefs about ourselves.

Curiously, these patterns of negative thinking frequently serve as the root cause of social anxiety. Inner dialogues dominated by phrases like "I'm incapable," "I'm inadequate," or "no one cares" can consume our attention, crippling our ability to fully engage with others. The consequences of such detrimental thinking can manifest in various ways, subtly undermining our social skills and creating barriers to genuine connection.

Signs of Negative Thinking

To better understand and address the effect of negative thinking on your life, it is crucial to familiarize yourself

PEOPLE PERSON | 39

with the common signs related to social interactions. By recognizing these telltale indicators, you can take the initial stride towards overcoming negative thought patterns.

So, let's dive in.

Withdrawal From Social Engagements

Sometimes our minds can go down a bit of a negative spiral, right? We end up assuming the worst, both about what other folks might think of us, and what might happen in the future. It's like having these little nagging thoughts that say, "Everyone thinks I'm weird" or "I'm just gonna make a fool of myself if I go to the party"– these can make us dodge social events altogether. And what's worse? We end up telling ourselves, "Well, people would probably have more fun without me around, anyway."

Then there's this thing called overgeneralization. This is when we have one bad experience and then we start thinking that all future experiences will be just as bad. It's like putting unnecessary restrictions on our lives. Let's say, for instance, you had a super awkward moment at a coworker's party. If you start believing that all future hangouts are going to end in the same embarrassing way, no matter how improbable that might be, then you're falling into the trap of overgeneralization. This often leads to withdrawal from social engagements.

Difficulty With Social Interactions

Negative thinking can make you nervous and apprehensive about interacting with others. A common instance of this is the phenomenon known as emotional reasoning, a cognitive distortion where your feelings are mistakenly considered the truth.

In practical terms, when you experience anxiety in a social setting, emotional reasoning may lead you to believe there's a genuine threat. This misperception can amplify your nervousness and act as a barrier to meaningful communication with others. While emotions are critical, they aren't always a reliable reflection of our surroundings.

Damaging Relationships

Negative thinking can really trip us up. It can fill us with doubt and kick off some not-so-great behaviors, like:

- Pointing fingers and blaming others
- Blowing situations way out of proportion
- Getting stuck in the past, mulling over what could've been

- Constantly chasing after other people's approval
- Dodging tough conversations in our relationships

These actions can lead to a lot of self-criticisms and make us hesitant to form new, meaningful bonds. Plus, it can put a strain on the relationships we already have with our family, friends, or partners.

OVERCOMING NEGATIVE THOUGHT PATTERNS

Your mental outlook acts like a lens through which you perceive the world. If the lens is primarily tinted with negativity, it can color all aspects of your life, from health to career, family, and beyond. Negative thinking can act like a snowball rolling down a hill, picking up more and more negativity as it rolls along.

Fortunately, with patience and consistency, you can gradually retrain your mind by using straightforward techniques.

Let's dig into a few techniques and learn how to ditch negativity!

Make Time for Negative Thoughts

Now I know this may seem like a contradiction and counterproductive, but allow me to explain. Knowing that you'll have dedicated time during the day to reflect on your negative thoughts helps reduce the time spent ruminating throughout the course of your day. When a negative thought comes up, write it down. At the end of your day, take 10 minutes to sit and go over the negative thoughts. In time, you will gain control over your negative thinking, and it will stop.

Become Your Own Cheerleader

Being your own cheerleader can be a game-changer. Offering yourself the same encouragement, kindness, and support that you would give to your best friend can transform how you navigate challenges.

It can be tough, especially on those days when everything seems to go wrong, and life feels like an uphill battle. But remember, it's on the tough days that being your own biggest cheerleader is needed the most.

Keep in mind, we often judge ourselves more harshly than we judge others. This self-criticism creates a persistent inner critic, making it hard to acknowledge our own growth and appreciate ourselves as we should.

So, even on the roughest days, it's important to continue supporting and rooting for yourself.

Reframe Negative Thoughts

Reframing negative thoughts is a powerful strategy to shift your perspective from negativity to positivity. It involves recognizing your negative thought pattern, challenging its accuracy, and replacing it with a more constructive thought.

For instance, if you frequently think, "I'm not good enough," you might reframe this thought to, "I'm always learning and improving." This process helps develop a healthier and more balanced outlook, reducing stress and promoting overall well-being.

Remember, it's a skill that gets better with practice. It's about gradually changing your thinking to foster a more positive mindset.

Turn To Your Journal

You're already going to be employing the journal method to help yourself recount negative thoughts you'd experienced throughout your day. This is essentially the same thing. Just be sure that you journal the thought as soon as it pops into your head and remind yourself that you will get to it later. Be sure to write down why the negative thought was present. Untangling your mind from negative thoughts is essential. Otherwise, you may end up operating at only a fraction of your true potential, or even less.

Establish New Hobbies and Incorporate Mindfulness

Mindfulness is something you're hearing a lot because people have rediscovered its power. Being mindful involves having an undying awareness of things to be grateful for, things that could have been worse, things you can do to improve your mood and attitude towards others, and more. It helps individuals remain conscious of themselves and those around them, which is an essential part of neutralizing negative thoughts.

It can be incorporated with daily meditation, where you'll make the time to calm and empty your mind of ruminating thoughts, as well as give your body much needed care. Yoga and other forms of physical activities can also help you break free from the cycle of negativity. Find what works for you and remain disciplined in performing them.

Daily Affirmations

Think of daily affirmations as little love notes to yourself, helping to kick-start your day with positivity and a vibrant can-do spirit! These empowering nuggets of positivity can be your secret weapon, creating a joyful rhythm for your day and reminding you of your strength and potential in every moment.

Each morning, go to your mirror, smile, and recite your daily affirmations.

Examples:

- I am the architect of my life; I build its foundation and choose its contents.
- My ability to conquer challenges is limitless; my potential to succeed is infinite.
- I am in charge of how I feel, and today I choose happiness.
- I trust that I am on the right path and am exactly where I need to be.
- My mind is full of brilliant ideas that I can execute.

Avoid Negative Morning News

It may seem like terrible advice, but trust me, it'll do you so much good.

Research found that starting your day with as little as three minutes of bad news can significantly affect the quality of your day. Watching negative news in the morning increases the chances of a negative perception and programs the mind to see only the downsides of situations (Forbes Coaches Council, 2016). Good news has the opposite effect, so perhaps listen to motivational speakers or affirmation music in the morning.

Gratitude Is Key

Contentment is only achievable when we're grateful for the things we have. There's nothing wrong with wanting to improve your life, but failing to be grateful for what you have means that no matter what you attain, it'll never be enough. Challenges and failures turn into learning opportunities, rather than mere setbacks, when you have gratitude. Regularly list the things you are grateful for, as this will help you focus on the brighter side of life.

WE ARE HARDWIRED FOR NEGATIVITY

As part of our human nature, we possess a tendency known as the negativity bias, which means we're more likely to pay attention to and ruminate on unpleasant experiences. In other words, we often react more strongly to criticism than to praise, an effect recognized as the *negativity bias* or *positive-negative asymmetry* (Cherry, 2022).

This bias signifies that instances causing us embarrassment or discomfort tend to linger in our minds longer than those that bring joy and satisfaction. For example, consider a time when you gave a presentation. People might have praised your eloquence and well-structured content, but one person said your slides were dull. Despite the mostly positive feedback, you find yourself fixated on one criticism, completely overshadowing the compliments. This is a classic example of our innate tendency to focus on the negatives at the expense of the positives.

Research Findings

Studies have shown that when trying to understand the world, people often lean towards the negative over the positive in various psychological contexts (Cherry, 2022).

Here's what we usually do:

- We give more attention to negative events compared to positive ones.
- We learn more from negative results and experiences.
- Our decisions are often influenced more by negative information than positive information.

It's the "unpleasant aspects" that capture our attention, linger in our memories, and, most times, shape our choices.

Consider the question: How can we cope with unwanted memories that unexpectedly come to mind? This, too, is influenced by our negative bias.

The field of psychology suggests that negative bias also affects our motivation to accomplish tasks. People are less motivated when a reward is presented as something to be gained, compared to when the same reward is framed as a way to avoid losing something.

This can affect your drive to achieve a goal. Instead of concentrating on what you'll gain by persistently working towards a target, you're more inclined to ponder on what you might have to relinquish to reach that goal.

Acceptance of Bad Versus Good News

Research findings have consistently revealed an intriguing tendency among individuals to readily embrace bad news compared to good news. This inclination arises from a heightened skepticism towards positive information, while negative news is quickly acknowledged as truth. Moreover, the abundance of negative news in the media contributes to a perception of its greater reliability. Hence, it is not surprising that unfavorable news often captures more attention in our collective consciousness.

Drive and Determination

Experts have found that human beings have the innate tendency to prefer the avoidance of loss as opposed to the potential of gain (Cherry, 2022). This means that even when presented with an opportunity that could greatly benefit them, their drive and determination come more from trying to prevent a negative outcome, rather than taking a chance on the possible positive outcome. Hence, the fear of negative effects is a much more powerful form of motivation than the possibility of positive ones.

Understanding our innate bias towards loss avoidance gives us power. It allows us to reassess our motivations when new opportunities arise. Instead of being hindered by the fear of negative outcomes, we can consciously shift our focus towards potential gains. This can lead to an empowering change of perspective. So next time, remember to step into opportunities with positivity and an open mind, embracing the potential for growth and progress.

The Origin of Negative Bias

Our predisposition to focus more on negative aspects and neglect positive ones probably has its roots in evolution. In the early days of human history, being vigilant about threats and potential dangers was crucial for survival. Individuals who were more alert to harmful situations and who dedicated more attention to negative elements were more likely to stay alive.

This increased their chances of passing on their genes, which would have made their descendants more alert to danger. In this way, our ancestors' need for survival may have hard-wired us to be more aware of negativity.

How It Develops

Infants have shown a stronger connection to the positive encounters, tones, and emotions of those around them, in contrast to adults and older children. They remember who brings joy and pleasantry better than those who don't. As they near the one-year mark (and sometime sooner), the proclivity to observe more negativity increases, and of course, the more frequently it does, the more ingrained it becomes.

In fact, it's been proven that negative information triggers a significant increase in the activity within a crucial region of the brain responsible for processing information, resulting in our actions and perceptions typically being influenced more strongly by adverse news, experiences, and data.

This has profound effects on how we perceive others, on our relationships, and on our decision-making process.

Effects of Negative Bias

Decision-Making

Decision-making is a constant in life, something we all inevitably engage in. It's common to find yourself reflecting excessively on whether you've made the right decisions in various scenarios, often driven by the fear of potential negatives. This fear-laden focus can significantly affect risk-taking capabilities and can lead to suboptimal decision-making. By dwelling too much on possible adverse outcomes, you might hold yourself back from wonderful opportunities, all because of fear.

Impression of Others

When evaluating whether to establish a closer relationship with others, the human brain has a tendency to focus on their negative attributes. Despite the presence of numerous positive qualities, it is often the negative ones that become ingrained in our minds and cause us to feel hesitant about pursuing a connection.

Personal Associations

Negativity bias often leads people to presume the worst in others, which can cause preemptively expecting a negative reaction from a partner or friend in a situation. This can lead to defensive conversations, arguments, and ultimately, resentment.

It's important to remember that negative comments leave a stronger impression than positive ones, especially in relationships. To counteract this bias, it is crucial to be aware of our propensity to dwell on negativity. By acknowledging this inherent human inclination, we can attempt to give others the benefit of the doubt and avoid constantly expecting the worst. This can ultimately lead to more positive and fulfilling relationships.

Overcoming Negative Bias

It's obvious that the negativity bias can have a negative impact on your well-being and life.

Fortunately, you can take measures to improve your outlook and fight this innate tendency.

Here are a few strategies.

- **Change your perspective**:

When entering a room or social setting, it's important to consciously change how you view the situation. Instead of dwelling on the reasons you may not want to be there, attempt to shift your perspective. Mentally list the positive aspects: the individuals who make these experiences more enjoyable, the delicious food, the uplifting music, and other delightful elements.

- **Be kinder to yourself**:

Nurturing self-kindness is a transformative practice. Treat yourself with the compassion you would give a friend, celebrating your successes and accepting your imperfections. Embracing self-kindness cultivates a positive mindset that enhances personal well-being and radiates outward to positively affect your relationships with yourself and others.

- **Treasure the present**:

Since positive experiences require more effort to be remembered, it's crucial to devote extra attention to the good that occurs in your life. Unlike negative events that might swiftly imprint on your long-term memory, you need to put in more effort to solidify joyous moments in the same way. So, when you experience something delightful, take the time to really absorb it. Replay the moment several times in your mind and relish the fantastic emotions that the memory elicits.

PRACTICING SELF-COMPASSION

Do you long for a kinder and more accepting relationship with yourself? Imagine creating an inner sanctuary of warmth and resilience, gracefully guiding you through life's challenges.

Self-compassion, which can be understood through its three dimensions of self-kindness, common humanity, and mindfulness, allows us to extend compassion towards ourselves (Graebner, 2021). It involves recognizing and acknowledging our own pain while embracing a gentle and non-judgmental attitude. Developing the ability to nurture a kind, loving, and accepting relationship with ourselves, even during difficult times, is a fundamental aspect of self-compassion.

While many people struggle with self-compassion, the encouraging news is that this skill can be learned and refined with practice. Just like any new skill, repetition and dedication are essential for it to become ingrained in our lives.

Learning Self-Compassion

The good news is that self-compassion is a learnable skill. Start your journey by trying the following self-compassion activities. They will help you cultivate self-kindness, strengthen your self-connection, and foster a compassionate mindset. Embracing these practices lays the groundwork for your ongoing self-compassion journey and its positive impact on your well-being.

Expand Your Emotional Range

This will involve actively being aware of the different emotions you experience and categorizing them accordingly. Doing this allows you to see what is significant to you and opens the gateway to better self-awareness. Once you know how certain things make you feel and why, you can then work on refining how you perceive them. If something upsets you and you're aware of it soon enough, you can prevent yourself from spiraling into a chain of dark thoughts by offering yourself reasons it's not as bad as it seems.

Improve Your Ability to Focus on the Present

As discussed earlier, this can only be achieved when you train yourself to always remain mindful. Mindfulness makes it possible to override negative internal monologues and appreciate the small things life offers. It will take some time, but you'll start noticing the difference once you've gotten the hang of it.

Reinvent Your Inner Critic

Most of our inner critics have been developed to help us remain cautious; however, many of the things it tells us are negative because we've already cultivated its negative outlook. Instead of encouraging you to take a risk that could better your life, it may persuade you not to even bother because you likely won't be successful.

By reinventing your critic and envisioning it as a person or character in your life, you start to take back power over it and can reimagine its purpose. Rather than allowing it to feed you negative what-ifs, you can flip it to feed you positive what-ifs.

Get a Growth Mindset

Self-compassionate people have a more realistic view of themselves. They're aware of their weaknesses and ready to work toward fixing them. Self-compassion should first stimulate the motivation to better yourself. It reinforces the belief that improvement is possible, and that effort will lead to success.

Reframe Your View on Mistakes

Embracing a fresh mindset regarding mistakes can speed up your learning and personal growth. Instead of relentlessly pursuing perfection, it's crucial to acknowledge that making mistakes is natural. By accepting your imperfections, you foster a more compassionate and forgiving outlook towards yourself and others. This newfound attitude grants you the freedom to learn from your mistakes and quickly move forward.

Be a Friend to Yourself Friend

When you witness someone close to you obsessing over a mistake they've made, it's natural to offer words of comfort and encouragement. However, when it comes to your own mistakes, you're quick to belittle yourself and engage in negative self-talk. Remember to extend the same kindness and patience to yourself that you offer to others. You hold the power to control the inner critic that lives within you.

If left unchecked, negative self-talk can have harmful consequences on your mental health and overall well-being. It can lead to feelings of isolation, anxiety, and other severe mental health issues. By learning to speak to yourself in a more positive way, you can begin to break the cycle of self-degradation and move towards a happier, healthier version of yourself.

So, make a conscious effort to be kind to yourself and take control of your inner critic.

EXERCISE: STOPPING NEGATIVE THINKING

This exercise helps you learn how to overcome negative thought patterns. You should try to engage in this exercise daily and gradually reduce it to three-to-four times weekly.

To begin, grab a journal or diary and create the following headings on a page:

- The negative thought I am having is…
- Is this thought true?
- What's the worst-case scenario?

- What's the best-case scenario?
- Is this thought caused by something else?
- Am I blaming someone else?
- Am I jumping to conclusions?

After a few hours have passed since you've answered these questions, revisit them and reflect on your responses. This practice will allow you to grain greater insight into the accuracy of your thoughts and enable you to identify when you might be falling into negative patterns. Over time, it will help you overcome them and create a more positive mindset.

ACTION STEPS

Use these action steps to help you foster greater positivity in your life:

- **Step 1:** Try to be open and confident in social settings and new situations, like at a business conference, a coffee shop, or at a party.
- **Step 2**: Practice positive self-talk and motivate yourself in social settings.
- **Step 3**: Acknowledge the difference between negative bias and choosing to be negative.
- **Step 4**: Use affirmations and gratitude journaling to focus on positives.

- **Step 5**: Practice self-compassion.

In this chapter, we focused on identifying and overcoming negative thoughts. In the following chapter, we'll look at stepping out of your comfort zone to improve social skills.

3

GETTING OUT OF YOUR SHELL

E mma *(not her real name)* used to feel trapped in her own world, isolated and hesitant to engage with others because of social anxiety.

With the support of a mentor, Emma embarked on a life-changing journey. Emma was gradually exposed to social situations, helping her build confidence and challenge her negative thoughts. As Emma's belief in herself grew, she rebuilt her relationships with family and friends and discovered a passion for art. Through ongoing support, Emma flourished, embracing volunteer work and becoming a confident and vibrant member of her community. Today, Emma radiates fulfillment and joy, having turned her life around from isolation to connection and purpose.

In this chapter, we explore the vital link between confidence and communication, providing practical guidance to establish and strengthen this connection.

SELF-ESTEEM AND COMMUNICATION

Self-esteem is not something we're born with, but something that develops over time based on several factors. Sadly, over 85% of people on the planet are said to have low self-esteem (Self-esteem, n.d.).

A clear sign of low self-esteem is having no faith in your own abilities or identity. People frequently endure feelings of disappointment and low self-worth when they feel they must meet the high expectations they've set for themselves.

Low self-esteem can have a profound impact on happiness, relationships, and performance in various areas of life. It can lead to increased anxiety, feelings of loneliness, and an inability to reach one's full potential, which can significantly affect the quality of your mental health.

Questions to Ask if You Suspect You Have Self-Esteem Issues

Want to know if you may have a problem with self-esteem? Consider these questions:

- Do most of your self-evaluations end negatively?
- Do the things your inner critic tells you make you view yourself in a less positive way?
- Do you blame yourself for all the mistakes you make?
- Does your self-doubt or feelings of inadequacy make you question whether you deserve happiness?
- Are most of your assessments on your achievements in life and physical appearance negative?

If you answered yes to at least three out of the five questions, then there is a good chance that you have a self-esteem issue, or you are extremely critical of yourself. But don't worry. The rest of this chapter is dedicated to equipping you with strategies to overcome these challenges.

First, let's learn more about self-esteem.

Self-Esteem and Social Competence

Low self-esteem can make communication difficult and can increase social anxiety. But how does self-worth affect communication, and how can it be improved?

Think about it. If you are always self-critical and believe that you aren't worthy, you'll have a hard time expressing yourself to others, which is exactly what we do when we communicate.

If you've been suffering from a lack of self-esteem or inadequate communication skills for a long time, you may have already noticed how various aspects of your life have been affected. Not only your interpersonal relationships, but also your professional growth. There may have been opportunities for promotion or an expansion of your responsibilities that passed you by, simply because you weren't able to cease the moment. *seize*

That said, ineffective communication isn't always because of low self-esteem. Correspondingly, low self-esteem isn't necessarily coupled with poor communication. Further, only you know if self-esteem is something you struggle with, but if you're still unsure, revisit the questions you answered above and really be honest with yourself when answering them.

If you conclude that you do in fact have this problem, understand that it's essential for you to work towards overcoming it.

Poor Self-Esteem and Communication Problems

The connection between self-esteem and communication is closely intertwined. Low self-esteem can contribute to difficulties in communication, and conversely, challenges in communication can affect self-esteem. By understanding this link, we can explore strategies to improve both self-esteem and communication skills, fostering greater confidence and effectiveness in our interactions.

Confidence and Communication

Individuals with high self-esteem often possess the important trait of assertiveness, which involves expressing one's thoughts and desires openly. Assertiveness and self-esteem have a positive connection, and both play a role in developing effective communication skills.

Assertiveness is a valuable quality in daily life as it empowers you to communicate confidently, express your needs directly, and say "no" when necessary. Individuals with low self-esteem may struggle to assert themselves and find it challenging to decline requests from others. Without assertiveness, one can become overwhelmed by others' demands and feel taken advantage of. Assertiveness is a form of self-care that establishes a balance between considering others' needs while respecting one's own individuality and thoughts.

By cultivating a healthy level of assertiveness and self-esteem, you enhance your communication skills, gain respect from others, and boost self-confidence and happiness.

When you know how to effectively utilize your assertiveness in a manner that is meaningful but still cordial, your communication skills are improved, and this undoubtedly leaves you with a greater sense of happiness.

Modelling to Become a Better Communicator

Find an inspiring person and follow their lead. This might seem like an odd thing to do, but you'll only need to do it until you've developed your own style and abilities. Observe the behaviors and traits of someone you already know to be self-assured and use what stands out to you about their approach to cultivate your own.

Interview them if you can. Pose hypothetical scenarios for them to answer, like how they'd respond, who they'd speak to, or what they'd do in certain situations and take from that what works for you. Next, try to put what you've learned into practice and test its efficacy.

Additionally, pay attention to their body language when engaging with others. How attentively do they appear to listen to those around them? How frequently do they offer visible signs of interest? In which situations do they employ formal or informal cadences?

Treating the development of your communication skills as a research-based experiment will help ensure you cover every aspect of what makes communication great.

BUILDING SELF-CONFIDENCE

Self-confidence is the belief in your abilities and worth, which allows you to face challenges and pursue goals with assurance and resilience.

A person with self-confidence:

- acts in alignment with their convictions, even if it goes against the majority
- embraces risks and ventures into the unknown
- acknowledges and grows from their mistakes
- graciously accepts compliments
- maintains an optimistic outlook

At some point in our lives, we all struggle with self-confidence to varying degrees. Self-confidence, or the lack thereof, manifests in various ways, and the journey of building confidence is a continual process for all of us.

Tips to Build Self Confidence

- Engage in positive self-talk
- Establish achievable goals
- Recognize and reaffirm your personal strengths and talents regularly
- Create lists of your accomplishments and moment of pride in your life
- Dedicate time to your hobbies and explore new interests to discover your passion
- Seek guidance from a counselor or mental health professional to learn effective self-management strategies for building confidence and self-esteem

The Importance of Having Confidence in Communication

How we convey our thoughts and ideas can determine whether others perceive us as credible and trustworthy.

Let's imagine you're in a high-stakes meeting, seeking to secure a major client for your company. As you articulate the benefits and value of your services, it becomes apparent that you lack confidence in your own words. Your voice trembles, your delivery lacks assertiveness, and doubts creep into your speech. In contrast, picture another professional in the same meeting confidently presenting a track record of successful client engagements, accompanied by glowing testimonials and concrete results. The stark contrast between the two approaches is striking. The individual who exudes confidence captivates the room and likely secures the new client.

The same principle applies to the realm of online product reviews. We've all come across those websites that simply regurgitate a few tidbits from the manufacturer's description, aiming to lure us into clicking so they can reap the financial rewards. However, their lackluster approach pales in comparison to someone who has genuinely experienced the product. Picture a review backed up by vivid videos or images showcasing a real person using and endorsing the item. The confidence exuded in such content is palpable, instilling trust and assurance in what is conveyed.

Confident communication in our personal lives holds tremendous power as well. Picture yourself engaged in a heartfelt conversation with a loved one or a close friend. As you express your thoughts, doubts, or emotions, you find yourself unsure and faltering in your delivery. Your voice trails off, and your body language betrays a lack of conviction.

Now, consider the alternative. Imagine speaking with unwavering confidence, your voice clear and strong, your words resonating with genuine belief and sincerity. Your loved one listens intently, captivated by your conviction and authenticity. They can't help but be drawn to your unfaltering faith in what you say, trusting in your words and finding solace in your steadfast presence.

Confidence in communication is the invisible thread that weaves trust, credibility, and genuine connection. It's a force that transcends professional boundaries, leaving a lasting impression on both our work and personal interactions. When we speak with conviction, we empower our words with an unwavering belief, capturing the attention and respect of those around us.

Overcoming a Lack of Self-Confidence in Communication

Our level of confidence isn't just about sounding impressive or making a good impression on others; it's about building the kind of relationships that can help us thrive.

One of the best pieces of advice I can give you is to really listen when someone is talking to you. I mean, truly give them your full attention and soak in everything they're saying. It's only when we're fully present in the conversation that we can respond honestly and selflessly.

It's so easy to get caught up in our own thoughts and start planning what we want to say next while the other person is talking. But that's where we go wrong. We need to break that habit and show genuine interest in what the other person is saying. Ask them questions about what they just shared, dive deeper into their thoughts and ideas.

And here's a little secret: people love talking about themselves. So, by being an attentive listener and showing genuine curiosity, you'll not only boost your confidence in communication but also make the other person feel valued and heard. It's a win-win!

Here are a few other strategies to help build your confidence.

- **Relax and embrace your true self**.

Avoid putting undue pressure on yourself and speak authentically. Resist the temptation to mimic others or use unfamiliar language to impress those around you.

Embrace your unique communication style and don't strive for perfection. When you accept yourself, you'll be more comfortable and confident in your ability to connect with others.

- **Maintaining good eye contact during conversations is important.**

Consciously making an effort to maintain eye contact can be challenging, especially if you're not used to doing it. Yet, by consistently practicing this skill, you will eventually become more confident in your communication abilities.

- **In discussions, steer clear of closed questions that elicit only simple yes or no responses.**

Instead, employ open-ended questions that encourage more elaborate and engaging answers, resulting in more captivating conversations. For instance, rather than asking, "Did you enjoy that movie?" which prompts a brief response, try asking, "What did you think of that movie?" or "What part did you enjoy most about that movie?" Open-ended questions often begin with words like "What," "Why," "Where," "When," "How," and allow for deeper exploration and discussion.

Remember that not every person will be compatible, and not all interactions will go perfectly. Accept this reality and recognize that others' opinions do not define your identity. Embrace mistakes as valuable learning experiences and move forward.

Confidence in communication grows through experience, so the key to improvement is practicing more. The more you engage in communication, the better and more self-assured you will become. It involves facing your fears and taking action despite them.

BECOMING A CONFIDENT COMMUNICATOR

Practice improves communication for everyone, regardless of confidence. Good communication entails both clearly expressing your views, listening to others, and reaching a common understanding.

Therefore, in this last section, we'll discuss quick strategies that you can use immediately.

- **Be prepared**:

When you are prepared, you can clearly and confidently articulate your thoughts and ideas. Before stepping into a situation, know your audience (when possible), gather relevant information, organize your thoughts, and anticipate potential questions or challenges. Practice delivering your message or presentation. By being prepared, you show professionalism, enhance your credibility, and ensure that the proper information is conveyed effectively.

- **Believe in yourself**:

Having faith in your capabilities can make a significant impact. Developing greater self-assurance will elevate your overall confidence. Believing in your unique talents, knowledge, and potential goes hand in hand with cultivating a sense of certainty. This inner conviction will radiate in your communication, masking any signs of nervousness, and leaving others unaware of any initial apprehension you may have felt.

- **Break free from comfort zones**:

Challenge yourself to step outside of your comfort zone. While it may feel intimidating, pushing beyond your limits is the most effective way to build your confidence. You'll be amazed at how quickly daunting tasks can become familiar and effortless through a bit of courage and perseverance.

- **Be approachable**:

Creating an atmosphere of approachability is key to establishing effective communication. Work on emitting a warm and welcoming presence that invites others to engage with you. This is accomplished by being open-minded, attentive, and non-intimidating in your interactions. By fostering an environment of approachability, you encourage individuals to freely express their thoughts, concerns, and perspectives. This builds trust, facilitates collaborative dialogue, and enhances the overall quality of interpersonal relationships.

- **Mind your body language**:

Learn to embody confidence. By projecting an image of assurance, you can actually cultivate a genuine sense of confidence when communicating. Pay attention to your posture, maintain eye contact, wear a smile, and allow yourself a moment of pause before speaking. These intentional actions can contribute to an enhanced sense of confidence and make a noticeable difference in how you present yourself.

- **Ask Questions**:

Asking clarifying questions helps you gain better understanding and shows that you're an active participant in the conversation.

- **Be Assertive:**

Assertive communication involves expressing yourself confidently, respecting others, and effectively conveying your thoughts, feelings, and needs. It is important to find the balance between assertiveness and respect, ensuring that you express your views without disregarding or belittling others. By navigating this fine line, you can maintain healthy relationships while still advocating for yourself in a confident and respectful manner.

- **Be Empathetic**:

When you show empathy towards others, it reflects your emotional resilience and strength. Enhancing this quality in communication not only fosters mutual respect but also enables you to better comprehend individuals with differing viewpoints. By developing empathy, you create an atmosphere of understanding and build meaningful connections, fostering harmonious relationships in both personal and professional settings.

- **Listen**:

Listening is a cornerstone of effective communication. It involves not only hearing the words being spoken, but also actively seeking to understand the meaning and emotions behind them. By truly listening, you show respect and validation to the speaker, fostering a sense of trust and openness. Listening allows for clearer comprehension, better collaboration, and the building of deeper connections.

CONFIDENCE EXERCISES

Ready to level up your confidence? Practice makes perfect, and I've got just the activities to help you on your journey. Get ready to boost your self-assurance with these empowering exercises. Dive in and level up!

Smile

Did you know that smiling has a remarkable effect on communication and can boost confidence? It's fascinating how even in a conversation, people can sense different smiles in your voice. And here's the surprising part: whether your smile is genuine or forced, it can still have a positive impact on your well-being. Research has shown that people who put on a smile, even if it's not initially genuine, experience lower heart rates and reduced stress levels. So, let that smile shine, even if it takes a little effort–you'll not only brighten your day but also enhance your communication with others.

The Power of Posture

Did you know that your posture has the power to boost your confidence? It's true! The way you carry yourself physically can actually influence how you feel mentally and emotionally. When you stand tall with good posture, you send a signal to your brain that you are confident and capable. So, whether you're sitting at your desk or walking into a room, remember to straighten up, pull your shoulders back, and embrace the power of a confident posture. It's a simple yet effective way to enhance your self-assurance and make a positive impression on others.

Create a Playlist

Creating a playlist is an effective way to improve your mood and boost your self-confidence. Music has been shown to enhance motivation, productivity, and self-esteem (Ye, 2021). In fact, studies conducted in 2014 indicate that specific songs, particularly those with heavy bass, can make listeners feel more empowered and confident.

When you're feeling low or struggling with confidence, turn to your favorite tunes and create a playlist. Choose songs that make you feel energized, inspired, and empowered to face the day. As you listen, your mood can be instantaneously elevated, giving you the confidence boost you need to tackle any challenge.

In essence, creating a playlist is an easy way to lift your spirits, make you feel more comfortable, and build your confidence. So next time you need a boost, make your go-to playlist and let the music work its magic.

Adopt an Alter Ego

Have you ever considered adopting an alter ego to boost your confidence? It might sound a little outlandish, but many successful individuals swear by this technique. By creating an alter ego, you can tap into a different persona that embodies the qualities and traits you aspire to possess. It allows you to step out of your comfort zone and take on new challenges with a sense of empowerment. Whether it's a fictional character, a role model, or even a version of yourself with an amplified persona, embracing an alter ego can help you overcome self-doubt and unlock your true potential. So, why not give it a try? Channel your alter ego's confidence and watch as you conquer obstacles and achieve remarkable feats you never thought possible.

Confidence Partners

Having a confidence partner is a great way to boost your self-confidence and enhance your relationships with others. Essentially, a confidence partner is someone who supports you and makes you feel good, and in return, you do the same for them. This partner could be a close friend, family member, or colleague who encourages you to be your best self and builds your confidence.

It's important to remember that this type of relationship is a two-way street. Just as your confidence partner supports you, you should also support them, offering kind words and encouragement when they need it. Don't hesitate to show your appreciation for their support and engage in open conversations about your shared confidence journey.

Ultimately, having a confidence partner helps you recognize your self-worth and feel more connected to others, both of which can boost your confidence and improve your overall sense of well-being.

ACTION STEPS

Now that we have covered all the content, use these action steps to help you master self-confidence:

- **Step 1**: Identify the connection between communication and self-confidence.
- **Step 2**: Be prepared to ask questions and practice your communication skills.
- **Step 3**: Emulate the communication styles of those you admire, but always be yourself.
- **Step 4**: Maintain eye contact and good posture when speaking.
- **Step 5**: Push play on your go-to playlist before social interactions to boost confidence.

Throughout chapter 3, we focused on stepping out of your comfort zone by building self-confidence through communication. In the next chapter, we'll dive into the fascinating world of body language.

4

EVERYONE IS ALWAYS COMMUNICATING—EVEN WITHOUT WORDS

Have you ever felt a conversation hitting a dead end, even though words are being exchanged? You might have noticed the other person's eyes frequently wandering to their phone, or perhaps they simply seemed disinterested.

Well, this experience offers a glimpse into the vast and silent sea of nonverbal communication.

Believe it or not, the essence of communication stretches far beyond our words. In fact, we humans have a remarkable capacity to convey and interpret meaning without uttering a single syllable. Remember sensing a romantic interest in someone even before they said anything? That's the power of nonverbal cues.

Unlocking the power of nonverbal communication can revolutionize the way you connect with others. It's like having a decoder ring for human behavior, enabling you to understand intentions, emotions, and responses more profoundly.

In this chapter, we will delve deep into the rich world of nonverbal communication.

NONVERBAL COMMUNICATION

Nonverbal communication is a fascinating aspect of human interaction. It's all about conveying messages without uttering a single word. We do this through hand gestures, facial expressions, body movements, and various other cues. Sometimes, these cues are unconscious and happen without us even realizing it, but they can also be deliberate.

Here's the thing: nonverbal signals can be incredibly powerful, and they can either support or contradict what we're saying verbally. It's crucial to understand how to interpret these cues to avoid misunderstandings and improve communication. Plus, your body language plays a significant role in how others perceive you and the message you're trying to convey. Interestingly, people tend to trust nonverbal communication more than verbal communication because they believe it reveals our true intentions.

That's why it's vital to be mindful of your nonverbal communication. Paying attention to the signals you're sending can make a world of difference in how effectively you connect with others.

How Important It Is to Pay Attention to Nonverbal Communication

Nonverbal communication comprises of a variety of things, like how you move, look at, listen, and respond to people to show sincerity, attentiveness, and interest. Nonverbal cues that match verbal communications foster and enhance trust and allow you to build rapport with the person you're speaking to.

It can serve the following five purposes:

- **Accenting**: Used to highlight or augment what is being said. You can accentuate your argument in several ways, e.g., thrusting your hands in the air can accentuate frustration.
- **Complementing**: Nonverbal communication complements what you say by enhancing or adding to it. For instance, giving a child an

encouraging smile after they've successfully completed a task shows approval and praise.

- **Contradiction**: By contradicting the message you're trying to convey, nonverbal communication might give the wrong message, showing that you're not telling the truth.
- **Repetition**: Nonverbal communication repeats what you're expressing verbally and frequently reinforces it.
- **Substitution**: When we communicate without using words, the message conveyed can be the same as if it were spoken verbally. In fact, it can be far more expressive.

Therefore, the power of nonverbal communication cannot be understated. It not only brings vibrancy and depth to our conversations, emphasizing key points and lending an air of authenticity, but it can also have its downsides. It's a double-edged sword that requires careful handling.

Let's take a closer look.

Can Nonverbal Communication Go Wrong?

To effectively align your body language with your true feelings and intentions requires a conscious effort. It's common for emotions and thoughts to go unchecked, but being mindful of your nonverbal cues is essential. While in informal interactions, body language often happens naturally as a response to your feelings, it becomes a more intentional act when you aim to shape others' perceptions or express yourself purposefully.

However, it's important to remember that body language isn't foolproof and can be subject to misinterpretation. If you struggle with social anxiety, managing your body language effectively may pose a challenge.

Nonetheless, it's crucial for you to place importance on being aware of the nonverbal cues you send and accurately interpreting those you receive.

Drawbacks of Nonverbal Communication

Relying solely on body language and nonverbal cues does come with the risk of relaying the wrong message. This misunderstanding can significantly affect the effectiveness of your communication and the connection you intend to build with those you're communicating with. It can cause a lack of trust or permanent distance between you and the other person.

Consider these scenarios to identify the negative aspects of inefficient nonverbal communication.

Jacob's Story

Jacob's co-workers shared a common sentiment: he radiated an intimidating, somewhat unapproachable aura. This stemmed from his nonverbal cues. First, his stern, seldom-smiling countenance often made colleagues feel scrutinized, adding a layer of tension to interactions. Second, his minimalistic, direct style of speaking, while not strictly nonverbal, contributed to his intimidating image, leaving room for misinterpretation. Last, his need for an exaggerated amount of personal space signaled standoffishness, making him appear less approachable.

Despite his unwavering job dedication, these nonverbal behaviors inhibited Jacob's growth opportunities, demonstrating how powerful silent communication can be in shaping perceptions and professional relationships.

Amelia's Story

Amelia is undeniably charming and has no trouble catching the eye of potential partners, but she struggles to build lasting relationships. She's an engaging character, often the life of the party with her witty humor. Yet, despite her constant laughter and bright smile, there's an aura of unease about her. Her hands were often tightly clenched, her gaze darted around, and her laughter was often a tad too loud. Her body was rigid with nervous energy, which made those around her feel on edge. Being in Amelia's presence often evoked a sense of tension, overshadowing her endearing qualities. Despite her great personality, Amelia's unintended projection of anxiety hampered her chances of nurturing a deep and meaningful relationship.

Tyron's Story

Tyron seemed like the perfect guy; ambitious, good-looking, and outgoing. However, after a few conversations, people found he was very opinionated and showed little interest in or patience for the ideas of others. He had a terrible habit of interrupting people as they spoke and wasn't a good listener. Those he spoke to felt ignored or disregarded and he couldn't build quality relationships with the people he admired most.

These scenarios vividly demonstrate the importance of mastering nonverbal communication. By being aware of and effectively using body language, you can ensure that your message is conveyed clearly, avoid potential mix-ups, and cultivate strong, trusting relationships in both your work and social life. Enhancing your skills in nonverbal communication can truly make a significant difference in your ability to get your point across and build meaningful connections.

TYPES OF NONVERBAL COMMUNICATION

We're about to explore nine distinct types of nonverbal communication that, while wordless, speak volumes about thoughts, feelings, and intentions. Each type serves as a unique channel that enriches interactions, making them more meaningful and impactful. Whether navigating personal relationships or professional ties, understanding these nonverbal cues can be your secret superpower.

Paralinguistics

Although paralinguistics forms part of vocal communication, it does not entail any actual language. It comprises vocal elements like volume, pitch, cadence, and emphasis. These elements may seem insignificant on their own, but consider how the intended meaning of a statement can be affected using different vocal elements.

For instance, you can detect passive aggressiveness or sarcasm. These subtle cues add layers of meaning to spoken words, helping us interpret the message correctly and gain a deeper understanding of the speaker's intent.

Gestures

Gestures, whether intentional or habitual, play a significant role in nonverbal communication. They are powerful tools that people often rely on to express themselves. Hand gestures, such as pointing, waving, air punches, and thumbs-up signals, are commonly used and carry specific meanings. However, it's essential to be mindful of cultural norms and context when using gestures to avoid misinterpretation.

Posture and Body Language

Posture, a vital aspect of body language, communicates thoughts, emotions, and attitudes. It reveals confidence, engagement, and emotional states. A tall, upright posture signifies confidence, while a slouched or turned-away position shows disinterest. Posture also reflects engagement: leaning in shows attentiveness, while a slumped stance implies disengagement. Additionally, posture reveals emotions, such as tense postures denoting stress and relaxed postures suggesting ease. Being aware of posture enhances communication skills and helps interpret others' unspoken messages.

Material Articles

The physical elements in our environment also play a role in nonverbal communication. These encompass visual elements and objects that align with an individual's message. For instance, when trying to make a point, someone may utilize relevant items or visuals to bolster their argument.

Moreover, the objects present in our personal spaces, such as our homes or offices, can offer insights into our interests and personality. They provide nonverbal cues about our identity and values. By attentively observing the material articles in someone's surroundings, we can gain a deeper understanding of their message, personality, and what truly matters to them. This understanding enables us to engage with them in a more meaningful way.

Proxemics

Personal space is an example of proxemics that people often discuss being necessary to help them feel at ease and true to themselves around others.

The amount of personal space a person feels they need and the amount they feel they are influenced by various factors, including cultural norms, societal expectations, and individual personality traits. Understanding these factors can help navigate social situations and adjust behavior accordingly. Understanding proxemics and personal space can also provide valuable insights into the dynamics of relationships.

Eye Contact

The comfort level with eye contact varies among individuals due to various factors like cultural norms, personal traits, and environmental influences. Interestingly, when we encounter something or someone we find attractive, our pupils enlarge, and we blink more frequently. Conversely, our eyes can also reveal emotions like fear, hostility, disappointment, and love.

Eye contact can also be used as a method to gauge a person's honesty. However, accurately assessing truthfulness through eye contact often requires the expertise of a skilled observer who specializes in this form of communication and understands the contextual cues involved.

Haptics

Haptics, or the use of touch as communication, is another important part of communicating. The way someone touches you may suggest many things, such as empathy, compassion, and sexual attraction, to name a few. Women tend to favor haptics to express emotions that relate to nurturing or affection. Men, on the other hand, tend to use it to show dominion over another person.

Appearance

The way we present ourselves physically to the world is a powerful form of nonverbal communication that can have a significant impact on how others perceive us. For instance, studies have shown that the colors we choose to dress in can not only impact our own psychology but also influence the opinions that others form of us (Cherry, 2023).

Additionally, research indicates that individuals who fit the conventional beauty archetype are more likely to benefit when it comes to employment opportunities and higher salaries. This underscores the importance of considering physical appearance as a nonverbal communication tool, particularly in professional contexts.

By being aware of how our physical appearance may be perceived by others, we can use it strategically to convey professionalism, confidence, and competence. This can be achieved through careful attention to our grooming, clothing choices, and overall presentation.

Facial Expressions

Your face also conveys nonverbal cues when communicating and, in most cases, these expressions are involuntary. They come in the form of macro or micro expressions. Macro expressions can last anywhere between half a second to four seconds and are more visible than micro expressions, which don't exceed half a second. Observing the facial expressions of the person you're speaking to can provide insight into what they're feeling, thinking, or trying to convey, making it an essential aspect of communication.

Examples

Have a look at the following examples of nonverbal communication:

- Raised hands: This could be a sign of exasperation or aversion

- Prolonged eye contact: This could be a sign of interest or desire to strike up a conversation
- Hand on arm: This can convey endearment or kindness
- Louder voice: This can show passion or excitement
- Smiling: This can show warmth, friendliness, or happiness
- Frantic hand waving: This can display frustration or anger
- Raised fist: This can show aggression or a sign of determination
- Eye rolls: This can suggest irritation, boredom, or dismissing what is being said
- Leaning in close: This might that imply you're listening attentively or have a sincere interest in what's being discussed
- Hug, fist-bump, handshake: These can be used to greet and sow affection

Nonverbal communication plays a vital role in how we connect with others and form meaningful relationships. The many types of nonverbal cues, such as body language, facial expressions, and vocal intonations, can convey a rich meaning that often complements or contradicts verbal communication. By becoming more aware of nonverbal cues and leveraging them strategically, we can improve our communication skills, strengthen our relationships, and deepen our understanding of the world around us.

EMOTIONAL AWARENESS

Emotional awareness describes one's capacity to identify and interpret one's own emotions and that of others.

The level of awareness is a big component of emotional intelligence. Emotional intelligence encompasses the ability to navigate life's challenges through a deep understanding of emotions, like managing your own emotional state and lifting others' spirits when they're down.

The five kinds of emotional awareness are:

1. Bodily sensation (a racing heart)
2. Action tendencies (crying)
3. Single emotion (sadness)
4. Blend of emotions (feeling sad and relief)
5. Blends of Blends of emotions (feeling sadness and relief while a partner feels shock and guilt)

If you have high emotional awareness, you're more adept at learning from your feelings rather quickly. For instance, if you're feeling sad, you can introspect to understand why and take steps to address it.

Those with heightened emotional awareness often experience greater joy and fulfillment. Understanding what makes you feel good, and what doesn't, empowers you to pursue the former.

The Connection Between Body Language and Emotional Intelligence

Emotional awareness, as we now understand, is a component of emotional intelligence. The other components include self-management, social awareness, and relationship management. Given that body language makes up more than half of all communication, it is crucial to be particularly attuned to it.

Each aspect of emotional intelligence plays an important role in body language. Let's look at each.

- **Self-awareness:** Paying attention to aspects like your tone of voice and posture can ensure that you convey your message suitably, matching the specific context of the situation.
- **Self-management**: Observing and appropriately adjusting your body language in response to evolving circumstances.

- **Relationship management**: Managing relationships with people and human interaction.
- **Social awareness**: Adapting your body language and tailoring your message to suit the dynamics of the situation.

HOW TO READ PEOPLE

Reading a person is an essential skill in communicating. Though it's true that some people are genuinely difficult to read, there are similarities in body language that can help identify what a person is thinking or saying.

Understanding how to classify body language cues as micropositives (being good emotions, words, or actions) or micronegatives (being bad emotions, words, or actions) is necessary for reading people.

Micropositives cues indicate interest or curiosity, while anxiety, indifference, or boredom indicate micronegative cues.

In a conversation, you want to see more micropositives than micronegatives. Asking yourself whether a nonverbal cue is positive or negative is the secret to interpreting any nonverbal cue.

Six of the most important body language cues are listed below.

Guilt and Shame Gestures

A common reaction humans display when they feel shame or embarrassment is straightforward to observe. Often, individuals in such situations instinctively touch the side of their forehead. Typically, it shows a desire to shield oneself or make the situation disappear. If the embarrassment intensifies, the subtle forehead touch could transform to covering the eyes entirely.

The Head Slant

Tilting the head to uncover the ear usually indicates an attempt to better hear what's being said. It is considered a micropositive and is a sign that you're actively engaged in the conversation.

Blocking

When an individual experiences feelings of disconnection, unease, or defensiveness, their body language may exhibit signs of blocking behavior, which is characterized by a distinct micronegative. Blocking typically involves the instinctive act of shielding a part of the body, creating a physical barrier between oneself and another person. This defensive posture is often subtle and emerges from a subconscious desire for self-protection.

Covering of the Mouth

Often, you'll notice that when a person lies, they unconsciously place a hand over their mouth. This gesture stems from a subconscious impulse. Mouth blocking is also used unconsciously when withholding a secret. It is also a reflexive reaction to embarrassment.

Facial Expression

Facial expressions hold a wealth of information and can serve as both micropositives and micronegatives. Interpreting facial expressions can significantly enhance one's ability to read people accurately. The ones to keep an eye out for are fear, happiness, contempt, surprise, sadness, and disgust. They are the silent telltale signs that reveal a person's genuine emotions.

Hands

Hand gestures offer valuable insights when attempting to decipher someone's thoughts. By observing how people use their hands while speaking (or not speaking), you can gauge their level of comfort, openness, or nervousness. For instance, fluid and expressive gestures often signal confidence and engagement, while fidgety movements might show discomfort. Hand gestures, as discussed previously, are also used to convey thoughts and emotions without words. By tuning into these subtle cues, you can significantly enhance your ability to read people.

Raised Eyebrow

The eyebrow lift is a subtle yet significant micropositive that often goes unnoticed in our nonverbal communication. Whenever we feel captivated, curious, or intrigued by something, our eyebrows naturally rise, allowing us to fully engage with our environment. This movement clears the way for a better view and invites us to explore the world around us with greater enthusiasm and energy. Despite being a small gesture, the eyebrow lift conveys a wealth of information about our inner state, making it a crucial aspect of nonverbal communication.

As we wrap up this chapter, you now have a glimpse into the captivating world of nonverbal communication. The awareness of feeling disconnected in a conversation due to subtle nonverbal cues reminds us of the profound impact they have on our interactions. With this knowledge in hand, you have the opportunity to unlock a deeper level of understanding and connection with others. By continuing to explore this rich realm, you will gain invaluable insights into human behavior and enhance your ability to forge meaningful connections.

ACTION STEPS

Now that we have covered all the content, use these action steps to help you master the art of body language:

- **Step 1**: Practice emotional awareness: notice how you feel during social interactions.
- **Step 2**: Identify which of the five kinds of emotional awareness you are experiencing.
- **Step 3**: Begin noticing your body language during social interactions.
- **Step 4**: Use the tips in this chapter to improve your body language in social interactions.

- **Step 5**: Begin noticing the body language of others and what it could mean.

Throughout this chapter, we uncovered the rich world of nonverbal communication and have explored its many facets, unmasking the subtle intricacies of body language and the way it shapes our interactions. Now, as we move into the next chapter, we'll shift our attention to another critical component of effective communication: active listening. By becoming better listeners, we can deepen our connections with others, gain valuable insights, and develop greater empathy and understanding.

SPREADING THE WORD

"All problems exist in the absence of a good conversation."

— THOMAS LEONARD

Did you feel like you were the only one who had this problem with social situations?

I'd hazard a guess that it's felt that way sometimes. One of the things that makes it harder to keep a conversation going when you're plagued with overthinking is that you can't shake the idea that everyone else seems to find it easier.

We all have that one friend who seems to be at ease in any situation they're thrown into, and we're left marveling at how they seem to be able to charm anyone within just five minutes of conversation.

But they're the anomaly. Not everyone finds it that easy. In fact, there are a great many people out there who have just as much difficulty with social situations as you do. My goal is to help them... and I'd like to ask for your assistance.

You'd be pleased to know that doing this requires not one second of small talk. In fact, as much as your skills and confidence are growing, there's no need for you to use them at all quite yet. All I'd like to ask you to do is write a few sentences that will serve to get this book into the hands of other people who need it.

By leaving a review of this book on Amazon, you'll show new readers that they're not the only ones who struggle to keep a conversation going... and you'll point them in the direction of the help they need to improve their experience.

Simply by letting other readers know how this book has helped you and what they'll find inside, you'll show them exactly where they can find the help they're looking for.

Thank you so much for your support. I know how isolating this can feel, but I promise you, you're not alone – and together, we can help even more people.

Scan the QR code to leave your review on Amazon.

5

LISTENING TO UNDERSTAND

Maria, a manager at a nonprofit, often found her team members disengaged during meetings, and projects were frequently missing the mark. Despite having skilled and talented individuals on her team, something was amiss.

She decided to attend a workshop on effective communication where she discovered the concept of active listening. Intrigued, Maria put what she learned into practice. In her next meeting, instead of dictating tasks, she listened, asked follow-up questions, and validated her team members' ideas.

The change was remarkable. Team members felt heard and valued, which enhanced their engagement. Projects were executed with increased understanding, and the quality of work improved significantly.

This instance highlights the importance of active listening. By truly hearing and understanding her team members, Maria not only improved the work output but also fostered a more positive and engaged work environment.

ACTIVE LISTENING

We've all been in situations where we could sense the other person's mind wandering during the conversation. It's quite disheartening and feels disrespectful, especially when we're discussing matters of great importance.

In fact, research shows that the average listener only recalls approximately 50–25% of the information they've heard, although listening makes up 45% of communication (CSU Global, 2021).

If you're in a learning environment, a professional scenario, or a personal relationship, missing out on up to 75% of what's being said could lead to significant misunderstandings. This is where the power of active listening comes into play, helping to circumvent such issues.

What Exactly Is It?

Active listening is dedicating your focus to completely hear, comprehend, and remember the information being shared. It's about attempting to dissect what you hear, sifting through the intent, content, and emotions conveyed by the speaker. It calls for undivided attention.

Another crucial aspect of active listening is affirming to the speaker that you're engaged. Gestures, such as maintaining eye contact, offering verbal affirmations, and responding with thoughtful comments, can significantly contribute to creating an environment of effective communication.

Reasons Active Listening Is Crucial

Active listening is not just an act, but an investment. An investment in relationships, understanding, and effective communication. It's the catalyst that transforms casual conversations into meaningful exchanges, fosters empathy, and builds robust connections. Professionally, it paves the way for team collaboration, informed decision-making, and proactive problem solving. In personal settings, it bolsters trust, minimizes misunderstandings, and deepens bonds. Simply put, active listening is a vital ingredient in the recipe for successful communication, making interactions more fruitful and satisfying.

ACTIVE LISTENING CUES

Nonverbal

Now that we have a solid understanding of nonverbal communication cues as discussed in Chapter 4, let's dive into their specific role in active listening.

In this section, we'll explore the subtle yet impactful ways nonverbal cues contribute to effective and attentive listening. Each nonverbal gesture, whether it's a nod or a genuine smile, plays a vital role in showcasing our engagement in the conversation and establishing a stronger connection with the speaker. By recognizing and strategically incorporating these cues, we can enhance our listening skills and communicate more effectively.

- **Mirroring**:

Mirroring is when the listener subtly matches the speaker's body language, tone of voice, or speech patterns. It's a natural way we establish rapport and show empathy towards the speaker. When done sincerely and subtly, mirroring can make the speaker feel more understood and validated.

- **Eye Contact**:

As mentioned previously, maintaining eye contact with the speaker usually shows that you're engaged and attentive. However, an overly intense stare could feel uncomfortable, especially to those who are more reserved or apprehensive. Assessing the right amount of eye contact for each specific context is key. When combined with encouraging smiles and other nonverbal cues, eye contact fosters a supportive environment that empowers the speaker to openly share their thoughts.

- **Smile**:

A smile can serve an important purpose in conversations; it can reassure the speaker that the listener is fully engaged and absorbing the information. When paired with affirmative nods, smiles become an interesting language of their own. They convey not just understanding, but also agreement and appreciation for the speaker's thoughts, contributing to a positive exchange.

- **Distraction**:

Incessant fidgeting, time-keeping, or lack of eye contact are all telltale signs of distraction that indicate you're not fully present in the conversation. While it can be easy to become distracted by the many stimuli around us, it's crucial to avoid these pitfalls at all costs to maintain effective communication.

Verbal Cues

The practice of active listening goes beyond just hearing. It involves engaging with empathy, authenticity, and consistent positivity. But to truly excel at it, you need to develop specific interaction skills, primarily recognizing and using verbal cues. This is where we dive deeper, bringing these skills to light. Let's get into the nuts and bolts of verbal cues, a critical part of active listening.

Summarization

A good way to show attentiveness is to recap what the speaker said in your own words. It is simply recalling key points raised and allowing the speaker a chance to make corrections if needed.

Questioning

To demonstrate attentive engagement, the listener can pose pertinent questions or make observations that enhance or bring clarity to the speaker's overall message. Such engagement not only reassures the speaker of the listener's interest, but also deepens the conversation, emphasizing the value of the information shared.

Reflection

Reflection deepens understanding and fosters meaningful communication by acknowledging and responding to the speaker's thoughts and emotions. It involves actively listening and responding to the thoughts, feelings, or ideas shared by the speaker.

Clarification

Clarification is the act of asking open-ended questions to the speaker for a more comprehensive understanding of their message. By doing this, the speaker can elaborate on specific details, ensuring the listener's complete understanding and avoiding potential misunderstandings.

Encouraging

Encouraging is expressing genuine curiosity and keeping the speaker motivated to continue. It shows that you respect their perspective, even if it differs from yours. Use dynamic vocal inflection to keep the conversation lively. Offering fresh viewpoints and suggestions can spark new thoughts. A question like, "What was your manager's reaction in that situation?" can help maintain momentum.

Balancing

Balancing in active listening involves eliciting further details from the speaker to help them analyze their own emotions better. For instance, posing a question like, "Do you feel the discomfort outweighed the feeling of being disregarded?" can provide a clearer picture of the speaker's experience.

HOW TO ACTIVELY LISTEN

Active listening isn't just one thing; it comes in many forms, each with its own strengths. In this section, we'll explore the four types of active listening and how to improve your active listening skills. As you'll see, mastering these techniques can significantly enhance your relationships and interactions. Let's jump into the details and put active listening into action.

PEOPLE PERSON | 115

Different Types of Listening

There are four types of listening that you need to become aware of to be a good listener. They include:

- **Empathic listening:**

Used during personal or emotional conversations. For instance, when a friend shares a struggle they're facing, empathic listening involves immersing yourself in their experience. You aim to understand their feelings, perspectives, and underlying emotions. This approach places the focus squarely on the speaker, allowing them to express themselves fully while feeling heard, valued, and supported.

- **Critical listening:**

Used when making an informed decision is required. For example, in a business setting, when a team member is proposing a new strategy, critical listening helps analyze the logic, strengths, and potential weaknesses of the argument. The focus in critical listening is primarily on the content and its implications, rather than the speaker's emotions or perspectives. This type of listening enables decision-making based on a comprehensive understanding of the presented information.

- **Comprehensive listening:**

In comprehensive listening, the focus is on understanding information in its entirety, connecting the dots, and storing it for future use. This type of listening is commonly used in educational settings, like in a lecture or a workshop, where the listener is expected to grasp new concepts or learn new skills.

- **Appreciative listening:**

Appreciative listening is the act of listening for enjoyment, pleasure, or inspiration. It often happens when we engage with music, a motivational speech, a stirring storytelling session, or even the calming rhythm of nature. In this form of listening, the focus is less on the speaker and more on the experience evoked by what is being heard. The listener's goal is to immerse themselves in the auditory experience, appreciating the sounds, words, and emotions they invoke.

Improving Active Listening Skills

Active listening is a soft skill that needs cultivation and consistent practice. This section provides additional active listening techniques to aid in this developmental journey, enhancing not just your listening abilities but also your overall interpersonal skills.

Listen Without Judgment

Non-judgmental listening doesn't mean refraining from negative or positive thoughts, instead, it refers to the ongoing commentary in your own mind. Any thoughts you form, irrespective of their nature, about another's words can lead you to focus on your perspectives rather than their message.

Instead, try to listen with a non-judgmental mindset, setting aside any spontaneous thoughts that may emerge. Differences in viewpoints are perfectly normal, and as an active listener, your role isn't to concur, but to comprehend. Concentrating solely on the speaker's words fosters a deeper understanding of their perspectives, which is the core objective of active listening.

Take Advantage of Nonverbal Cues

In the process of active listening, your verbal responses are usually limited, making it crucial to use positive nonverbal cues to show support such as maintaining eye contact. Try to refrain from actions like crossing your arms or fidgeting. Where fitting, engage with a smile or a nod. As discussed previously, nonverbal cues not only affirm to the speaker that their message is being heard, but they also foster a more relaxed conversational environment.

Avoid Interrupting

During a lively conversation, it can be tempting to chime in with your thoughts or to expand on a point someone has just made. However, when actively listening, this isn't recommended.

In active listening, the aim is to focus completely on the speaker's words. Even though thoughts or responses may pop up as you listen, it's important to put them on hold. Maintain your focus on understanding the speaker's message.

Ask Open-Ended Questions

After the speaker completes their thoughts, display your engagement by asking open-ended questions. Avoid introducing your own assumptions into these questions.

For instance, you could ask:

- "Can you elaborate on…"
- "What inspired you to pursue that route?"
- "How did you feel later?"
- "What did you mean when you said…"
- "What can I help you with?"

EXAMPLES OF ACTIVE LISTENING IN CONVERSATIONS

Active listening might seem challenging if you're new to the concept. To help, let's walk through a couple of scenarios showing what to do and what not to do.

Example 1:

Mike: "I've been feeling really overwhelmed lately with the kids' remote learning."

Taurice: "You think you have it bad? My three kids have been driving me up the wall. I hardly get any work done!"

In this conversation, Taurice fails to demonstrate active listening. Rather than empathizing with Mike's situation or encouraging him to express more about his feelings, Taurice redirects the conversation toward his own experiences. This dismisses Mike's feelings and shifts the focus from Mike to

Taurice, which does not foster open and supportive communication.

Example 2:

Alex: "I've been really overwhelmed with the new project. There's a lot to do, and it feels like the deadline is rushing towards me."

Chris: "It sounds like you're under a lot of pressure with this project. The impending deadline is making things more stressful for you."

Alex: "Yes, exactly. And I'm also worried that I might not meet the expectations of the team."

Chris: "That's understandable. Facing a challenging project and feeling the need to meet your team's expectations can be overwhelming. Can you tell me more about the specific aspects that are causing you the most stress?"

In this dialogue, Chris reflects Alex's feelings, validating his experience, and then asks an open-ended question to better understand the issues Alex is facing. The focus remains on Alex's perspective and experiences, which are central to active listening.

Example 3:

Gina: "I've been really upset since I didn't get that promotion. I really thought I was the best candidate for the role."

Bella: "Oh, that's unfortunate. But you know what? I didn't get the promotion I wanted last year, too. I was so devastated. But then, I started working on this new project and things got really exciting."

Gina: "Right, but I worked really hard for this, and..."

Bella: "Absolutely, you need to keep working hard. But remember, not getting a promotion is not the end of the world. In fact, it could be the start of something new and exciting."

In this conversation, Bella does not effectively employ active listening. Instead of focusing on Gina's feelings and acknowledging her disappointment, Bella redirects the conversation to her own experiences. This can give the impression that Bella is not truly interested in what Gina is saying, and instead is more interested in discussing her own experiences. Furthermore, by offering unsolicited advice and downplaying Gina's feelings, Bella may make Gina feel unheard and dismissed. Active listening requires focusing on the speaker, validating their feelings, and refraining from making the conversation about oneself.

Example 4:

Nita: "Since I relocated for this new position, I've been wrestling with homesickness."

Margie: "It seems like you're struggling with the loss of familiarity and the comfort of home. That must be really challenging."

Nita: "Yea, it's definitely been a struggle. I miss my family and everything I was used to back at home."

Margie: "I can only imagine how tough it must be to adjust to a new environment away from your family and all the things you were accustomed to. What do you miss the most about home?"

Throughout this conversation, Margie employs effective active listening techniques. She acknowledges Nita's feelings of homesickness and empathizes with her circumstance. Rather than attempting to offer a quick solution or steer the conversation away, Margie encourages Nita to share more about her feelings, fostering an environment conducive to open and supportive communication.

The act of genuinely listening to understand holds immense power in shaping our relationships, communication dynamics, and overall experiences. When we actively engage with others, genuinely seeking to comprehend their perspectives and validate their emotions, we create an environment characterized by empathy, respect, and mutual understanding. Through the practice of active listening, we unlock the potential for deeper connections, meaningful collaborations, and effective problem-solving. Let us embrace the art of listening to understand, as it can enrich our lives and foster a world where communication flourishes and bridges are built.

ACTION STEPS

Here are practical steps you can take to cultivate and fine-tune your active listening skills:

- **Step 1**: Always lessen distractions when you're engaged in active listening.
- **Step 2**: Use nonverbal cues like eye contact to show that you are engaged.
- **Step 3**: Use verbal cues like questioning or summarizing to enhance understanding.
- **Step 5**: Model positive behavior to leave a lasting impression.
- **Step 5**: Begin noticing if listeners you're engaged with are actively listening when you speak.

In this chapter, we've unraveled the complexities of active listening, equipping you with vital communication tools. In Chapter 6, we'll elevate our conversation skills even further by delving deeper into the art and science of asking insightful questions, an integral complement to the principles we've discussed.

6

HOW DO YOU ASK THE RIGHT QUESTIONS?

I n our previous chapters, we touched on the role that thoughtful questioning plays in effective communication. However, given its paramount importance, it warrants a deeper, more detailed examination.

Questioning may sometimes feel like navigating a minefield. Too many questions might appear intrusive, while too few could show a lack of interest or understanding. Despite this balancing act, asking the right questions at the right time remains an integral part of any conversation.

Mastering this skill is not always straightforward. You might grapple with finding the right question, or struggle with articulating it in a way that opens productive dialogue. Yet, the effort invested in refining this skill can improve your ability to communicate tremendously.

So, in this chapter, we'll go deeper into the importance of questions, the characteristics of a good question, and how to ask meaningful ones.

THE IMPORTANCE OF ASKING QUESTIONS IN CONVERSATIONS–BEYOND THE OBVIOUS

While many people understand asking questions can help gain new information or clarify a misunderstanding, there are some lesser known, yet equally important, benefits of posing questions in conversations:

1. Questions as Bridge Builders: One of the powerful aspects of questioning is its ability to act as a bridge between people with differing viewpoints. When two individuals have conflicting perspectives, asking thoughtful and open-ended questions can help create a dialogue where each person seeks to understand the other. It creates an environment of empathy and respect, which is vital in resolving differences and fostering harmonious relationships.
2. Questions as Catalysts for Self-Reflection: The value of questions isn't only external. They

serve an important internal function as well. When we ask ourselves questions, we stimulate introspection and self-reflection. It allows us to dig deeper into our thoughts, emotions, and motivations, enhancing self-awareness and personal growth.

3. Questions as Engagement Tools: Asking questions also plays a key role in keeping conversations engaging and dynamic. A well-timed question can shift the energy of a conversation, re-engage a disinterested party, or add an unexpected layer of depth to a discussion. It keeps the conversation from becoming a monologue and ensures active participation from all parties.

4. Questions as Strategy Tools: In strategic situations such as negotiations or sales, asking the right questions can provide valuable insights into the needs, desires, or constraints of the other party. This can help tailor your approach or proposal in a way that addresses their concerns and achieves a favorable outcome.

5. Questions as Means of Expressing Humility: By asking questions, we admit that we do not know everything and are willing to learn from others. This expression of humility can be very

endearing and often leads to more open and honest exchanges.

Appreciating these diverse roles of questions can enrich our conversations and deepen our interpersonal relationships.

Why You Should Always Ask Questions

It's important to really drive home the importance of asking questions.

When you ask questions, you're communicating to the other party that their input holds value, and that their experiences, insights, or expertise are worthy of exploration. This act can significantly boost their self-confidence and promote more open, collaborative communication.

Furthermore, questions stimulate creative thinking. They encourage us to break away from routine thought patterns, encouraging innovation. A well-placed, insightful question can challenge preconceptions and inspire fresh perspectives. Moreover, questions act as a vehicle for continuous learning. Questions prompt discussions, serving as catalysts for the sharing of ideas, fostering mutual understanding and shared empathy. So, remember, every question you ask carries the potential to drive empowerment, stimulate creativity, inspire learning, and facilitate meaningful discourse.

QUESTION FORMULATION

Constructing the perfect question is a delicate art. And a crucial component is being conscious of your conversational goal. Questions should be shaped not only with the intent to gather information but also aligned with your objectives - whether to deepen understanding, foster collaboration, or challenge perspectives. Hence, mastering the skill of formulating meaningful, goal-oriented questions is essential for enhancing the quality of our interactions and maximizing the value derived from them.

The New Socratic Method

The New Socratic Method can be summarized as a more empathetic and emotionally intelligent approach to facilitating dialogues and learning.

It incorporates a set of guiding principles that shape the course of conversation, much like a code of conduct. Participants agree to suspend judgment, mostly question, and collaboratively engage. It also embraces a structured approach, through the steps of clarifying, examining, and calibrating. In the clarifying stage, the focus is on understanding the other person's viewpoint through detailed questioning. The examining phase is about delving deeper, challenging ideas, and testing the robustness of the viewpoint. Last, the calibrating stage is where the discussion is refined and adjusted based on the insights gathered in the previous stages.

Conversations are a collaborative endeavor, where the goal is to foster shared understanding rather than striving for personal victory or dominance.

The Importance of Conversational Goals

Conversational goals exist on a spectrum ranging from purely competitive to purely cooperative. On one end, competitive goals drive conversations where each party aims to "win" or achieve their own objectives, often at the expense of the other's. At the opposite end, cooperative goals guide interactions where parties work together towards a shared understanding or mutually beneficial outcome.

Understanding where your conversation lies on this spectrum can influence your approach and tactics.

Navigating competitive conversations brings unique challenges for both the one asking questions and the responder. The questioner might encounter resistance, as the other person might be reluctant to share information, and there is always the risk that they might resort to deceit. On the other hand, the responder faces the challenge of maintaining their strategic stance, as divulging too much puts them at a disadvantage.

In cooperative conversations, the dynamics shift. The questioner may find it difficult to draw out honest feedback or critical information, especially if the other person shies away from conflict or is hesitant to share bad news. As for the responder in cooperative conversations, the challenge lies in ensuring that the dialogue remains productive. It's all too easy to slip into comfort and forget to contribute to the conversation, hence thwarting the purpose of cooperative communication.

Tactics To Achieve Conversational Goals

Let's turn our attention to the specific tactics and strategies that can effectively guide us to our goals.

Tone Is Crucial

We briefly discussed this concept when we explored paralinguistics. Let's look at tone as it relates to question formulation. Tone can alter the meaning of words and tilt the conversation's direction. It can imply curiosity, concern, skepticism, or even hostility, regardless of the words used. It provides cues to the listener about your intentions, emotions, and attitude toward the topic and about them. Therefore, tactically employing tone can help manage conversational dynamics. A friendly tone can put someone at ease, encouraging openness and fostering a cooperative environment. On the other hand, a more assertive tone might exhibit authority or urgency in competitive scenarios. Therefore, mastering your tone can significantly affect how your questions are received and the quality of responses they elicit.

Pay Attention to Sequence

How you arrange your questions can be significantly influenced by the situation. In challenging dialogues, posing tough questions at the outset can pave the way for your conversation partner to be more receptive. Studies show that people are more open with sensitive details when asked in a sequence from the most intrusive to the least. Starting with a highly personal question, such as "Have you ever fantasized about hurting an animal?" makes the following questions like "Have you ever lied to your boss?" seem less intrusive in comparison, leading to more open responses. But be cautious, as an overly sensitive initial question could be off-putting. Hence, finding the right balance is key. For building relationships, a different approach is recommended — start with less personal questions and gradually escalate. It's also important to note that question sequencing can substantially shape the way people perceive and respond to the topics under discussion.

Ask Follow-Up Questions

Follow-up questions are like a secret weapon in a conversation. They don't need a lot of planning or thinking. They come up naturally as you talk, making the conversation flow easily. Not only that, but the speaker also feels respected and heard. Their simple yet strong impact highlights how important they are for good communication.

When to Use Open-Ended vs. Close-Ended Questions

Understanding when to use open or closed-ended questions can make a world of difference in your conversations. Open-ended questions have their strengths: they encourage dialogue, foster deeper understanding, and can lead to insightful discoveries. They are especially useful in situations where a comprehensive understanding is necessary, such as in brainstorming sessions or conflict resolution.

However, it's important to know that open-ended questions may not always be the optimal choice. In scenarios where you need specific information or a direct response, closed-ended questions are more efficient. They can help keep a conversation focused and concise, which is crucial in time-sensitive situations or when dealing with individuals who may become side-tracked easily.

On the flip side, closed-ended questions often restrict responses to a simple 'yes', 'no', or a selection from a predefined set of answers. While they can provide direct answers and clarity, they also risk stifling dialogue and could guide the conversation in a biased direction. Furthermore, they might prevent the emergence of nuanced or unexpected insights that could stem from more open discussions.

It's about balancing the two types of questions. This balance depends on the context, your goals for the conversation, and the dynamics of the relationship.

Group Dynamics

It's been observed that the presence of others can significantly affect an individual's willingness to answer questions, and people follow the lead of their peers. When individuals are led to believe that others are open and revealing, they're more likely to divulge sensitive information themselves, emphasizing the power of group influence.

However, a few guarded individuals in a group can cause a shift toward a more closed-off environment. Conversely, a single person's openness can encourage the rest of the group to share more freely (Brooks &

John, 2018). This highlights the importance of fostering an open and trustful atmosphere when conducting group conversations.

Interestingly, there are notable differences in perception between participants in a conversation and external observers. Participants appreciate being asked questions and often view the question-asker more favorably. However, from an observer's perspective, the individual responding to the questions often appears more engaging and memorable. This underscores the complexity of conversational dynamics and the importance of being mindful of how one's role in a conversation can shape the way they are perceived by others.

Strategic Answers

A conversation is like a game of chess, where each move plays a crucial role in shaping the direction of the game. Just as the questions we pose can build trust and promote information sharing, the way we respond can be equally strategic.

When responding to questions, it's like deciding on a chess move: we're constantly making choices between privacy and transparency. Do we move our pieces forward? How openly should we strategize? What's the plan when a question could expose a weak spot in our defenses, or put us at a strategic disadvantage? Both ends of the spectrum - absolute secrecy and total transparency - have their own benefits and drawbacks.

Privacy can act like a protective barrier, allowing room for innovation and learning. In a business negotiation, holding back key information, such as limited bargaining options, can help gain the upper hand. However, transparency, akin to a bold and open strategy in chess, is vital in forming meaningful alliances and relationships. In business negotiations, transparency can lead to mutually beneficial outcomes by unveiling aspects that are of low importance to one party but hold high value for the other.

However, maintaining secrets, much like hiding your strategy in a game, isn't without its downsides. Studies show that holding secrets during social interactions can lead to a constant recurrence of intrusive thoughts. Moreover, keeping secrets, even outside of social situations, can be mentally taxing, disrupt concentration and memory, and could even pose potential harm to long-term health and well-being.

In the corporate landscape, the default approach leans more towards preserving privacy, often underestimating the potential advantages of transparency. It's often a case of missed opportunities when realizing too late the deep connections could have been formed with a colleague, or the superior deals we could have negotiated once formalities are over, and candid conversation ensues.

To maximize the benefits and minimize the risks of responding to questions, it's pivotal to strategize in advance. Consider what information you're willing to share and what to keep private before engaging in any conversation. Much like in chess, a well-planned strategy can significantly affect the outcome.

QUESTION QUALITY

The knack for asking good questions isn't easy for everyone.

At first glance, it appears quite straightforward. But in reality, the fine art of asking great questions requires finesse and thoughtful cultivation. Chances are, there have been instances where a question you posed didn't quite hit the mark. But remember, that's all part of the learning process and you can hone this valuable skill.

Proficiency in posing the right questions, at the right time, is the lifeblood of fluid and productive conversations.

Good vs. Great

A good question serves as a conversation catalyst, opening pathways to new ideas and insights. It's clear, purposeful, and crafted in a way that encourages thoughtful and meaningful responses. By asking good questions, we facilitate smoother exchanges of ideas, promote mutual understanding, and drive the conversation toward achieving a desired outcome. Good questions can help us learn, clarify misunderstandings, and stimulate more in-depth discussions.

Once you've mastered asking good questions, take it a step further and learn to ask great questions takes. Great questions aren't just tools to keep the conversation going, but a key to unlocking profound insights and shifting perspectives. A great question dives into the deep end of the conversational pool, challenging assumptions and inviting a deeper exploration of underlying beliefs and feelings. It resonates on a personal level, igniting emotions and revealing sincere responses. A great question isn't just answered and forgotten, but lingers in the mind, provoking ongoing reflection and potentially unveiling new insights. Ultimately, while good questions advance the dialogue, great questions have the power to transform it.

What's a Good Question-Asker?

Being a good question-asker goes beyond the mere act of asking; it requires certain qualities to stand out.

Curiosity is a defining trait of a skilled question-asker. They possess an innate desire to explore beyond the surface and discover new information. Their questions go beyond the mundane and encourage deep thinking, prompting thoughtful and insightful responses from others.

Instead of settling for generic questions like "How was your day?", strive to delve deeper and elicit more meaningful answers by asking about specific moments or experiences, such as "What was your favorite part of today and why?"

Intentionality is another vital characteristic of a good question-asker. They understand the importance of preparation and purpose in their questioning. By carefully selecting their words and considering the timing of their inquiries, they ensure their questions serve a specific objective. Before asking a question, they reflect on why they are seeking the information and what insights they hope to gain from the response.

Last, bravery plays a significant role in effective question-asking. It takes courage to ask the right questions, even when they may challenge the status quo or provoke uncomfortable conversations. Many people stay away from asking certain questions due to fear of judgment or backlash. However, a good question-asker understands the value of seeking clarity and is unafraid to use their voice to ask tough questions, fostering growth and understanding.

How to Ask Better Questions

Now that you've learned the importance and significance of your questions, let's dive a little deeper into how to equip yourself with the knowledge of asking better, more important questions.

Here are tips to get you started on asking better questions.

Through Active Listening

As we've previously discussed, active listening is a crucial component of effective communication. This is especially true when it comes to constructing quality, impactful questions. The last thing you want is to ask about something that has already been thoroughly addressed, which can show disinterest to the speaker. Even with positive body language and other forms of nonverbal communication, asking these types of questions can undermine the rapport you've built. To avoid such missteps, make sure to actively listen to the speaker, ask insightful questions that reflect their contributions, and show your engagement in the conversation. By doing so, you'll deepen your understanding of the topic, showcase your interest to the speaker, and foster a productive dialogue.

Explore the Subject

Are you truly aware of the essence of your questions and their purpose? It may appear obvious, yet it is crucial to ensure that you clearly understand what you are asking. Pinpoint the precise aspects that you find perplexing or require further clarification. By honing in on the specific areas of confusion, you can sharpen the effectiveness of your questions and facilitate a more meaningful exchange of information.

Keep the following in mind:

- Does the setting call for an informal or formal approach when asking your question?
- Do you need an opinion or data?
- Do you know the answer, or will the answer surprise you?
- Is common ground or empathy what you're looking for?
- Are you seeking answers or explanations?

Go With the Flow

Most conversations periodically deviate from the principal subject. Relax, this is not a sign that something's gone wrong. It simply means you're succeeding in your quest to get the person to open up. Allow these shifts to take place and follow along as they go. If you still haven't received the answer you need, delicately steer the discussion back on course.

Make the Most of Silent Pauses

Embrace the moments of silence that occur during a conversation, rather than feeling uneasy about them. These brief pauses provide an opportunity to reflect on the questions you have asked and the responses you have received. Use this time to evaluate the overall progress of the conversation and consider how to delve deeper into well-crafted follow-up questions. Avoid the pressure to respond immediately and instead, make the most of these silent pauses by allowing yourself and others the space to think and gather their thoughts.

Keep Questions Short

Avoid lengthy dragged-out questions. Keep them concise and focused, providing enough context without overwhelming the listener. The goal is for the person you're asking to understand your question with one clear explanation, rather than repeating it multiple times. By practicing clarity and brevity, you can ensure effective communication and avoid confusion.

Avoid Leading Questions

Avoid using leading questions that already assume an answer. When you ask a leading question, you are often seeking confirmation of what you already believe. While this may be harmless in certain cases, it limits the opportunity for diverse responses and fresh insights. The true power of questions lies in discovering something new and gaining valuable perspectives. Strive to ask unbiased, clear, and straightforward questions that allow for a range of opinions and the possibility of learning something unexpected.

THE ROLE OF LANGUAGE

Language is the cornerstone of effective communication. It shapes our perception of the world and influences how we interpret and respond to the words of others. It is through language that we truly express ourselves and leave an indelible mark on those around us.

The Functions of Language in Its Most Simple Form

The basic function of language is to facilitate communication and convey meaning. It is the foundation upon which human interaction and understanding are built.

Language serves various fundamental functions that go beyond mere communication.

The informative function of language empowers us to convey information in a clear and concise manner, enabling effective knowledge sharing and understanding. Through language, we can inform, educate, and enlighten others by presenting facts, data, and explanations.

The expressive function of language is a powerful tool for self-expression, allowing us to convey our emotions, feelings, and attitudes to others and even to ourselves. It provides a means of articulating our joys, sorrows, desires, and beliefs, fostering emotional connection, and facilitating introspection.

In addition, language plays a vital directive function, enabling us to provide guidance, command, or instruction. Whether we are issuing instructions, giving orders, or guiding ourselves through decision-making, this function empowers us to direct our actions and navigate various situations effectively.

Elements of Language

Language is made up of six parts:

- **Clarity:** Using language that ensures the audience understands the speaker's message with ease and accuracy.
- **Economy:** Using only the essential and appropriate words to convey your message while eliminating any unnecessary language. It entails avoiding fluff and keeping your language straightforward and accessible.
- **Obscenity/Vulgarity:** The use of indecent or lewd language, which includes, but is not limited to, curse words and scathing remarks.
- **Jargon**: Refers to language used in specialized fields that the average person isn't familiar with. This might occur, for instance, in the medical, engineering, technological fields.
- **Power:** The utilization of words to exert control or influence over others, whether through manipulation, commanding actions, or achieving personal agendas. It can also involve

positioning oneself as an authoritative figure within a context or setting.

- **Variety:** This is a speaker's ability to use the range of elements to articulate ideas.

Language Styles

Language encompasses various styles that cater to the speaker's communication needs. While some styles may be influenced by a person's individuality, others are adapted to suit specific situations, even if they differ from the speaker's usual manner of speech.

Let's review a few.

Direct and Indirect

Direct communication is characterized by clear and straightforward expression. It leaves no room for confusion or misinterpretation. In this style, the speaker does not rely on hints, implications, or nonverbal cues. Indirect communication takes a less direct approach by expressing thoughts or desires in a non-explicit manner. It often involves the use of hints, implications, or nonverbal cues to convey the intended message.

Personal and Contextual

These two language styles encompass certain complexities. Personal style expresses an individual's individual characteristics. While contextual styles involve adapting one's language based on the specific context of a situation. For example, a mother might employ their personal style when speaking with relatives and friends, while utilizing a contextual style when delivering a presentation at work.

Untranslatable Words

Untranslatable words are words that don't have a direct equivalent in another language. They represent unique concepts, cultural nuances, or deep emotions that can be difficult to fully capture in translation. One example is the Japanese word "komorebi," which refers to the interplay of sunlight filtering through the leaves of trees.

Use Effective Language

For effective communication, using appropriate, vivid, and inclusive language can make a significant impact.

First, using appropriate language means tailoring your choice of words to suit your audience, which we've discussed previously. It's about finding a balance between being relatable and engaging while respecting their sensibilities.

Besides appropriateness, employing vivid language adds depth and richness to your communication. By using imagery, descriptive adjectives, or even onomatopoeia, you can paint a vivid picture in the minds of your listeners or readers.

Last, using inclusive language is essential for creating an inclusive and welcoming environment. It means using language that embraces and includes all individuals, regardless of their gender, race, or any other characteristic. By using inclusive pronouns like "they" instead of assuming a specific gender, and by avoiding any form of discriminatory language, you create an atmosphere of respect and acceptance.

As we conclude this chapter, we are reminded of the profound impact that effective questioning can have on our interactions and pursuit of knowledge. By developing the skill of asking thoughtful and relevant questions, we unlock new avenues of understanding, spark meaningful conversations, and uncover valuable insights. The ability to ask the right questions not only empowers us to navigate complex social situations but also cultivates curiosity and promotes lifelong learning. So, embrace the art of asking the right questions, as it serves as a catalyst for growth, discovery, and deeper connections with others and the world around us.

ACTION STEPS

Use these action steps to help you master good questioning:

- **Step 1**: Understand the importance of a good question in a conversation.
- **Step 2**: Know what kind of answer you are looking for.
- **Step 3**: Know when to ask open or close-ended questions.
- **Step 4**: Be a good listener and ask follow-up questions.
- **Step 5**: Use body language to convey a question effectively.

Throughout this chapter, we uncovered the significance of questions, their power, quality questions, and the role of language. In the next chapter, we will look at handling difficult people.

7

HANDLING HARD-TO-HANDLE PEOPLE

We've all encountered them - people who seem to have a knack for pushing our buttons and making conversations more challenging than they need to be. Whether it's the coworker who always shoots down your ideas or the family member who constantly stirs up conflicts at gatherings, dealing with difficult personalities can be quite the task. But fear not! In our exploration, we will uncover effective strategies to skillfully navigate interactions with hard-to-handle individuals, demonstrating grace and composure along the way.

WHAT MAKES SOMEONE A DIFFICULT PERSON?

Many of the interactions we have aren't necessarily a walk in the park, however, there are those that particularly stand out. It's the encounters with people whose uncongenial mannerism stays with you, even after leaving their company. These types of people are a part of life and unavoidable, unfortunately. They may be a classmate, a colleague, or even a family member.

Whoever it is, they have the innate ability to turn any interaction with them into misery and you'll only be able to avoid it for so long. Learning how to handle and communicate with these troublesome individuals will help with your interactions with them and will also help you prevent that person's negativity from affecting you.

What Makes a Person "Difficult"?

Everyone has a unique personality–quirks and all. However, personality clashes don't inherently result in difficult relationships. What usually causes the problems are criticism, poor communication, and a lack of empathy.

Criticism

Navigating interactions with individuals who exhibit a highly critical nature can be hard, given their tendency to maintain exceedingly high standards and readily pinpoint flaws in various aspects of life. The repercussions of their incessant critique can be especially distressing, particularly when the relationship is close-knit. Such dynamics can lead to significant emotional strain, as their pessimistic remarks and judgments have the potential to scar one's well-being and personal connections.

Poor Communication

Consistently interrupting you when you speak or disregarding your thoughts and opinions is another key trait. Their communication style may exhibit indirectness, passive-aggressiveness, or rudeness, making conversations with them anything but straightforward. The aftermath of such interactions often leaves one feeling dissatisfied.

Zero Empathy

Their limited ability to understand and acknowledge the emotions and circumstances of others can make them appear uncaring. Dealing with such individuals can be difficult as they struggle to grasp the perspectives and feelings of those around them, primarily prioritizing their own needs and interests above all else.

Identifying a Difficult Person

Whoever said that knowing is half the battle was right. While difficult people don't walk around with signs on their backs, there are telltale signs that you can look out for.

Below are a few indicators to help you identify these individuals:

- Most people steer clear of them
- They're excluded from important conversations
- They insult or belittle you
- Their behavior in public and private are different
- They show toxic traits and behaviors
- They always have all the answers
- They second guess everything you do and say
- You're uncomfortable around them
- They lack emotional regulation
- It's their way or the highway

Spending time around difficult people can affect your personal and professional relationships and will inevitably affect you. You should take precautions to avoid being affected by such detrimental behaviors. The first thing you should do is remember that this is who they are, and it's not your job to change or fix them.

HANDLING DIFFICULT PEOPLE

You can't escape them, unfortunately, so learning how to live alongside them is your best bet. There are strategies to help you navigate these situations and manage these difficult people with greater ease while helping to preserve your well-being.

- **Identify the type:**

This involves figuring out what kind of difficult person you're dealing with. They'll fall into one of four types.

- **The Yes-People.** These individuals don't want to step on anyone's toes or make waves. They're also known as Passives, Pushovers, and Weaklings. They contribute little to conversations or the people around them.
- **Tanks.** These individuals are known for being a loose cannon, bossy, or a handful. They want it their way and will do anything to get it.
- **Debbie Downer or Negative Nancy** are

156 | SANDY R. WILLIAMS

common nicknames afforded to pessimistic
people (Vanessa Van Edwards, n.d, para.4).
They're also known as Downers, and they always
have something bad to say. They're the whiners
of the group and are close to impossible to
please.

○ **Better Thans**. They're also known as One
Uppers, Know It Alls, or Show-Offs. They love
to name drop and compare to impress you.

• **Try understanding**:

In dealing with challenging individuals, it can be beneficial to understand their underlying motivations and
perspective. One effective approach is to identify their
core values and what truly matters to them. This
insight can shed light on their decision-making process
and help create a more understanding and open-
minded atmosphere. For instance, some individuals
may prioritize financial gain, while others may prioritize influence or knowledge. By acknowledging and
respecting their values, it becomes possible to navigate
conversations with greater ease and minimize potential
conflicts. This approach is useful when engaging with
assertive individuals (Tanks) who may appreciate the
opportunity to express their opinions and feel heard
without feeling the need to dominate or exert control.

- **Curb their toxicity**:

Dealing with challenging individuals can be a taxing experience, especially when they display toxic behavior characterized by passive-aggressiveness, meanness, or hurtful actions. In such situations, it's helpful to gain an understanding of their perspective while also prioritizing your well-being. Recognizing the detrimental impact of toxic relationships, it is crucial to establish boundaries and create a buffer zone to protect yourself. Surrounding yourself with supportive friends and minimizing the time spent in their presence can be effective strategies for preserving your emotional and mental health. Remember, your well-being is paramount, and prioritizing self-care is essential when dealing with toxic dynamics.

- **Don't try to change them**:

When faced with difficult people, whether they are part of our social circle or family, our initial response may be to try to change them. We might want to inspire more positivity in those who are pessimistic, encourage assertiveness in those who are passive, promote calmness in those who are confrontational, and foster humility in those who exhibit superiority. However, it is important to recognize that these attempts fail more times than not. Not only that, pushing someone to change can often lead to resentment, stubbornness, and a worsening of their behavior.

COMMUNICATING WITH DIFFICULT PEOPLE

Although effective communication is the key to getting the help we need, expressing ourselves, and establishing meaningful connections, difficult people make it a challenging endeavor.

Use the following tips to help lessen stress.

Communicating with Mr. or Ms. Right

Mr. or Ms. Right certainly believe they're right. So how do you communicate with someone like this? Determine the key factors necessary for someone to be considered "right" and use them to assess their credibility and validity.

- Evidence: Is there evidence to support their views?
- Objectivity: Is this an opinion or is it the truth?
- Possible Bias: Is there something that is clouding their judgment?

Are they open to having a two-way dialogue with you? If not, determine if it's worthwhile for you to continue to engage with them.

During an interaction, it's important to know when to disengage. Pull the plug on the conversation when:

- They are aggressive and you feel distressed.
- You're not given the opportunity to share your thoughts.
- They have a 'just because' attitude and don't provide evidence.

Communicating with someone who avoids vulnerability

Look into the reasons someone may be averse to vulnerability:

- The idea of vulnerability is scary because they don't feel safe.
- Vulnerability was not modeled for them growing up.
- It's not a behavior that they practice, so they're uncomfortable during conversations.

Encourage the person to be more vulnerable by expressing the underlying values and motivations behind your desire for a deeper connection. Also, create a safe and comfortable space for them to open up by understanding what makes them feel safe, whether it's being in a familiar environment or having a warm drink.

Approach the interaction with a gentle and warm curiosity, employing active listening, reflection, and empathy. This approach is more likely to help the person open up, compared to a rigid and interrogative line of questioning that could further close them off.

Last, modeling vulnerability by sharing your own experiences can facilitate a sense of safety, trust, and reciprocity. Acknowledge that vulnerability can be daunting for some individuals, and by demonstrating your own vulnerability, you can encourage a deeper level of connection and understanding.

Conversing With the Extremely Anxious and Fragile Type

Find a comfortable and calm time to have a conversation with the other person, avoiding any triggering statements like "We need to talk" or "I wanna chat later" that may cause anxiety. Instead, suggest hanging out and asking when would be a good time for them.

When addressing challenging topics, take the time to make the other person feel safe. Express your appreciation for them and remind them of their importance to you. Validate their struggles and acknowledge their growth and healing.

Be mindful of your language, avoiding accusatory or hostile words. Instead, use feeling words like "sad," "scared," or "angry" to express your emotions while taking ownership of your experience.

Frame the conversation positively, focusing on what you would like to see rather than dwelling on the negative. For example, instead of saying, "You never help me with the kids, and I feel unsupported," try saying, "I've been feeling overwhelmed with the kids lately, and it would mean a lot to me if we could divide the tasks. I appreciate how well you handle *bedtime* and would love it if you could take responsibility for that."

Remember, it is important to assert your needs and boundaries even when dealing with someone who may be fragile or anxious. Be sure to express yourself and prioritize your own well-being.

Communicating With Aggressive or Easily Irritated Individuals

Find a time that works well for both of you to have a conversation where you can both feel comfortable. It's important to choose a setting where you won't be easily interrupted or distracted, allowing you to focus on the discussion at hand.

Remember that each person is responsible for their own emotional reactions. You cannot make someone angry; it's their choice how they respond. Practice responding instead of reacting and be a role model by demonstrating the behavior you want to see in others. It's only fair to hold everyone to the same standard. Take note of situations or conversations that trigger reactive responses and approach them calmly and thoughtfully. Responding calmly when faced with someone's anger can help defuse tension and create a more constructive atmosphere.

Take the time to genuinely listen to your partner's needs and boundaries. Give them the space to express themselves fully and strive to understand their perspective. Sometimes restating what they've said in your own words can help ensure clarity and show that you are engaged in the conversation. For example, you could say, "I hear you, and it sounds like you're feeling..."

If emotions run high and someone becomes angry, let them know you acknowledge their feelings. However, if their anger or energy becomes counterproductive to the communication process, suggest taking a break and revisiting the conversation when emotions have settled. Allowing them to feel their emotions while creating space can pave the way for a more productive discussion later.

Remember, it's important to establish and uphold your own boundaries. If someone uses belittling or threatening language or exhibits disrespectful behavior, it's crucial to assert clear boundaries and communicate that such behavior is not acceptable. Your well-being and safety should always be a priority, and if necessary, remove yourself from the situation to ensure your own peace of mind.

OVERCOMING COMMUNICATING HURDLES WITH DIFFICULT PEOPLE

Sometimes they are strangers we meet on the train going to work. And sometimes they are our family and friends. Whoever they are, there are tools you can use to help navigate the hurdles you face when you communicate with difficult people.

Let's take a closer look.

- **Acknowledge your role**:

Accountability is important when you're trying to make someone see things from your perspective. The blame game solves nothing, so show the person that you accept responsibility for your own actions. This usually encourages people to do the same.

- **Full transparency**:

Honesty will always be the best policy. So many people think lying or sugarcoating the truth somehow makes things better. It doesn't. Full transparency allows you to display the characteristics you'd like them to see. Be specific in your discussion, meaning tell them what needs addressing, what you'd like the outcome to be, and how you think you guys can best achieve it. Make sure there's room for their opinions and ideas too.

- **Welcome criticism**:

Even though you're addressing something you'd like to work on in the other person, you're not perfect and will probably be reminded of. Don't jump on the defensive. Accept your flaws and agree to work on those that need it. Criticism doesn't have to be all bad. Use it as a tool that helps you improve and be the best version of yourself. That said, don't allow the other person to use this as a strategy to shift the focus onto you.

- **Avoid assumptions**:

Assuming what makes a person act the way they do only makes them more hostile and proves that the true intent behind your conversation is not to gain understanding, but to ostracize them for their flaws. Reserve all judgment and allow them to explain the reasons for their actions.

- **Keep an open mind**:

Your idea of what causes them to do what they do might be right, but it might also be wrong. Have the patience to see things from the perspective of others. You might find that you misinterpreted something that was said or done. Rather than try to get everyone on board with your speculations, hear others out and allow room for a fresh perspective.

MORE COMMUNICATION TIPS

Here are some more tips to improve communication with difficult people.

- **Stay cool, calm, and collected**: Emotions can run high in conversations with difficult people.

But do your best to stay as calm as possible and not let your emotions get the best of you.

- **Don't Judge**: We never know what a person is going through, or has gone through, that triggered a particular response. Give people the grace that you'd like given to you.
- **Don't take it personally**: It's sometimes hard not to take things personally with a difficult person. Take steps to understand their side and do your best to communicate your side.
- **Set boundaries**: Assert your boundaries. Stand up for yourself and maintain a healthy level of mutual respect in any conversation.
- **Don't reciprocate negativity or aggression**: Getting aggressive and negative won't get you the outcome you want.
- **Don't force compliance**: Avoid saying things like "take it easy" or "calm down" because telling someone what to do or how to act never works in these situations. Recognize that everyone has the right to their own feelings.
- **Maintain good personal space**: Be sure that there is more than enough personal space so that everyone feels safe and respected.
- **Employ help from others**: Involving a third party can be useful when the situation needs to be diffused or if need of an outside perspective.

We've explored the challenges and nuances of dealing with difficult people. Whether it's a combative coworker, a toxic family member, or a challenging friend, interacting with hard-to-handle people can be both emotionally draining and mentally exhausting. However, armed with practical strategies and a deeper understanding of how to navigate these tricky situations, you can emerge from even the most challenging interactions with grace and fortitude. By practicing the strategies discussed, you can foster positive relationships, maintain your peace of mind, and stay true to your values.

ACTION STEPS

Use these action steps to effectively navigate challenging interactions and master how to handle difficult people:

- **Step 1**: Identify what type of difficult person you're dealing with.
- **Step 2**: Don't try to change the person.
- **Step 3**: Avoid negativity and toxicity as best as possible. If need be, leave the conversation until later, when the person has calmed down.
- **Step 4**: Use empathy.
- **Step 5**: Above all, put your mental health first.

In this chapter, we explored effective strategies for navigating difficult people and engaging in constructive communication with them. Now, let's turn our attention to a different aspect of social interaction in the next chapter - small talk. We will delve into the skills and techniques that can help us start and maintain light-hearted conversations, fostering connections and creating meaningful interactions in various social settings.

8

PRACTICING SMALL TALK AND BEING GOOD AT IT

I magine stepping into a lively party, where the air is filled with laughter and music. As you stroll, you see a group engaged in conversation. Intrigued, you approach them with a warm smile and join the circle. The topics of discussion range from recent movies to favorite hobbies and weekend adventures. Eager to contribute, you share your thoughts on a newly released movie and ask about their thoughts on it. As the conversation unfolds, a sense of camaraderie and excitement engulfs the circle. Laughter echoes and stories are shared, creating an atmosphere of genuine connection and enjoyment. This small talk exchange exemplifies the magic of social gatherings, where seemingly insignificant conversations can blossom into unforgettable moments of shared joy and lasting friendships.

Small talk, like the other techniques discussed in this book, is a skill that takes practice but can be mastered. So, let's get to it!

MASTERING THE ART OF SMALL TALK

Small talk serves as a way to connect with others on a casual level, without going into deep conversations. It's used to discuss trivial and lighthearted subjects, filling silences, and fostering a sense of ease between individuals. Whether it's used during a party, in an elevator, or on a date, small talk can sometimes feel like a daunting task that leaves you anxious and uncomfortable.

Let's discover the keys to mastering this essential social skill.

Why Small Talk is a Big Deal

Small talk often gets a bad rap. People underestimate its importance, especially when it comes to simple topics like the weather. But trust me, it's a skill you want to have up your sleeve. Just think about all those times you engage in small talk throughout the day, whether it's with your loved ones or even with acquaintances.

Sure, chatting about the weather with family and friends seems like second nature. It's easy-peasy, right? But small talk goes way beyond that cozy circle. It's equally crucial in social and professional settings. I'm talking about those moments when you need to break the ice, establish connections, and build trust.

Think about it: when you strike up a conversation with someone you barely know, small talk acts as the bridge to deeper, more meaningful discussions. It's like a secret code that unlocks common interests and shared experiences. And finding that common ground is like striking gold. Suddenly, you're not just talking about the weather anymore—you're bonding over a shared love for hiking, music, or cooking.

But the best part is small talk doesn't just benefit your relationships; it can boost your happiness. Engaging in light-hearted conversations and connecting with others on a casual level is incredibly rewarding. It's a chance to grow socially, improve your communication skills, and feel a sense of belonging.

So, it's time to embrace those seemingly mundane conversations and watch as they open doors, create new connections, and bring a lot of joy into your life.

The Body Speaks in Its Own Language

In Chapter Four, we delved into the intricacies of body language and its powerful role in communication. Remembering those insights, it becomes easier to gauge whether someone is open to engaging in small talk or not. Pay attention to nonverbal cues like avoiding eye contact or displaying signs of impatience, such as fidgeting. These behaviors might show that starting a conversation with such individuals might not be the best idea.

On the flip side, keep an eye out for individuals who exhibit relaxed facial muscles, maintain eye contact, and wear a friendly smile. These are the people who are more likely to be receptive to small talk. By displaying similar signs, you create an inviting atmosphere and open the door for others to approach you for casual conversations.

So, note of the body language cues and be mindful of the signals you convey. It's all about creating a comfortable environment that encourages small talk and fosters connections with those around you.

All-Purpose Small Talk

With small talk, it's helpful to remember that some topics have universal appeal, making them suitable for any situation and anyone you're chatting with, and certain subjects work better in specific contexts. For instance, you might save work-related topics for conversations with coworkers in the office, while discussing hobbies among friends.

It's best to maintain a positive tone and avoid broaching "heavy" subjects, including anything negative or controversial that may spark disagreement among people.

While it's great to be engaging, try not to overwhelm the other person with random or out-of-the-blue questions. Instead, allow the conversation to flow naturally. Avoid firing off questions like you're ticking items off a list. The most successful small talk often stems from situational observations, where you notice something interesting about your surroundings and smoothly incorporate it into your conversation.

Here are more helpful tips:

- **Show enthusiasm**:

Instead of seeing small talk as potentially stressful, view it as an exciting opportunity to learn and connect with others. You never know who you might meet or what fascinating insights they might have to share. So, embrace the chance that every small talk interaction holds the potential for an amazing and enriching discussion.

- **Display attentiveness**:

This is once again where your active listening skills come into play. Just because it's small talk doesn't mean you should pay any less attention. Failing to show interest during small talk may make it difficult to have meaningful conversations with the person in the future.

- **Put your phone away**:

In this digital age, our phones have become a comforting shield, concealing our emotions, and providing solace when we feel socially uneasy. However, this constant attachment to our phones can unintentionally sabotage our ability to engage with others. When you're constantly engrossed in your phone, it creates an invisible barrier that deters people from approaching you. It sends a clear signal that you're preoccupied and disinterested, hindering the opportunity for genuine social connections. So, it's time to put down the security blanket and embrace the world around you.

- **Leave questions open**:

People enjoy talking about themselves, which sets the stage for good small talk. Open-ended questions encourage openness and allow the other person to share exactly how much they want, which can lead to follow-up questions.

SMALL TALK TOPICS

When it comes to small talk, the world is your conversational playground. From the latest movies and books to travel experiences, hobbies, and even local events, there's no shortage of intriguing topics to explore. Regardless of the situation, having a repertoire of small talk topics at your disposal can make social interactions more enjoyable and memorable. Don't let fear hold you back. It's time to embrace small talk and overcome any anxiety associated with it.

A great way to ease those nerves is by equipping yourself with the knowledge of exactly what to discuss and what to avoid. Understanding which topics to delve into and which ones to steer clear of can provide a sense of confidence and ease. So, instead of shying away from small talk, empower yourself by knowing the right things to say.

Small Talk Topic Ideas

Here are a few of the best small talk topics to consider.

- **Weather**:

While it may seem like discussing the weather is a cliché, it's actually a reliable and neutral topic that everyone can relate to. Whether a storm has recently passed or you're experiencing a heatwave, the weather provides an easy entry point for conversation.

Take a moment to observe your surroundings and use these simple weather-related phrases as conversation starters:

- "Beautiful day, isn't it?"
- "Looks like it's going to be a scorcher."

So, embrace the simplicity of discussing the weather and let it guide you into more engaging exchanges.

- **Arts and Entertainment**:

Arts and entertainments offer a plethora of topics for small talk, such as books, music, TV shows, movies, cultural events, and much more. You could discuss the current music scene, share your favorite songs or artists, and ask others about their go-to tunes or recent discoveries. The possibilities are endless.

Here are a few questions to jumpstart your small talk:

  - "Are there any podcasts you've been enjoying lately?"
  - "Have you come across any new apps or games that you'd recommend?"

Be aware of your conversation partner's knowledge of movies, TV shows, and books. Avoid diving into detailed plots or scenes if they haven't seen or read them. Look for common ground and focus on shared interests.

- **Food**:

Food can be a great small talk topic if you keep it light, positive, and neutral. You can dive into conversational about local eateries, seek recommendations, or even discuss the joy of cooking at home.

Here are a few small talk topics to get the conversation rolling:

- "Have you been to any new restaurants lately?"
- "What's your favorite cuisine?"

Remember, just like any small talk topic, it's essential to stay positive and avoid dwelling on dislikes or complaints about particular foods.

- **Family**:

For many of us, our families are our most prized possessions, and we jump in headfirst when given the opportunity to talk about them.

Small talk about family may include:

- "Do you have any siblings?"
- "How long have you been married?"

However, it's important to be mindful of potential sensitivities. For example, asking if someone has kids or plans to have kids can be tricky if they're dealing with infertility or personal challenges. However, if the other person brings it up, it's a green light to show genuine interest, so ask away.

- **Work:**

Work-related topics are another popular choice for small talk. It's common to be asked about your occupation or whether you enjoy it.

To start a conversation about work, you can use openers like:

- "What do you do for work?"
- "How long have you been in that profession?"

Remember to focus on learning about others and discussing topics that genuinely interest you.

- **Travel**:

Travel and vacations never fail to captivate people's attention. Many people enjoy talking about travel and sharing their experiences.

Consider these questions:

- "What's your favorite vacation destination?"
- "Do you have a specific travel destination on your bucket list?"

These questions can open new avenues of conversation into each other's travel aspirations and unique travel stories.

- **Sports**:

This topic can serve as great icebreakers for small talk. Keep track of which sports are played during different seasons.

You can state a conversation by asking something like:

  - "Did you catch the game last night?"
  - "Who's your favorite team?"

Avoid trash-talking and instead focus on discussing aspects like team or player performances to maintain a friendly conversation.

- **Hometown**:

Many people favor this topic. People love sharing their origins, traditions, and family stories. This topic can certainly grab their interest, steer the conversation, and might even surprise you to learn the backstories of people you thought you knew.

Try starting small talk with:

- "Are you from this area?"
- "Where are you originally from?"

It's good for you to share your hometown as it makes the conversation much more intimate and helps to solidify your connection.

- **Hobbies**:

People love talking about their hobbies and is a wonderful conversation starter.

Consider asking questions like:

- "What are some of your favorite hobbies that you enjoy in your free time?"
- "Have you picked up any new hobbies recently, or are there any you've been wanting to try?"

Approach the conversation with curiosity and respect and embrace the opportunity to learn from others.

Bad Small Talk Topics

Now that you know a few good small talk topics, it's equally important to be aware of topics that should be avoided.

Here are a few.

- **Politics and religion**:

It's wise to avoid topics that can lead to heated debates or strong differences of opinion, such as religion and politics. These subjects evoke powerful emotions and can quickly derail a friendly atmosphere.

- **Sex**:

Sex is inappropriate for small talk because of its intimate and personal nature. Talking openly about sex or using sexual innuendos should be avoided when talking to strangers.

- **Appearance**:

It's important to steer clear of questions related to appearance. Don't ask a person if they're pregnant (unless you know them), weight loss or gain, or any physical attributes. You never know the underlying reasons behind someone's appearance, and unintentionally putting them in an uncomfortable position can be avoided by respecting their privacy and personal boundaries.

- **Money**:

Discussing your own finances, as well as asking about someone else's, is highly inappropriate. You'll likely make people uncomfortable, and they'll avoid you in the future.

- **Discriminatory Humor:**

Engaging in sexist or racist jokes is offensive and a surefire way to abruptly end a conversation. It's important to note that sometimes people make jokes without realizing their potential to offend others. The rule of thumb is to exercise caution and refrain from jokes targeting a person based on race, culture, gender, or sexual orientation.

- **Personal Gossip**:

While discussing celebrity gossip can be acceptable in small talk, it's important to avoid gossiping about people you know personally. Engaging in gossip not only reflects negatively on you, but you risk others being connected to or aware of the individuals involved. Refraining from speaking ill of others can protect you from potential embarrassment and maintain a positive reputation.

In closing, avoid small talk topics that may be one-sided, such as specialized expertise or uncommon hobbies that your conversation partner may not be familiar with. While it's okay to mention these topics when relevant, keep the conversation more general and be mindful of others' interest levels.

Refrain from discussing past relationships, especially on first dates, as it can be off-putting and hinder future connections. Similarly, avoid discussing health issues, offering unsolicited advice, or delving into potentially sensitive health topics, as it can come across as intrusive. Instead, focus on creating a positive and inclusive small talk that respects others' boundaries and promotes enjoyable conversations.

ACTION STEPS

Now that we have covered all the content, use these action steps to help you master small talk:

- **Step 1**: Prepare, prepare, prepare! Have premeditated small talk topics in your mind before going into a social setting and remember to keep it light.
- **Step 2**: Practice, practice, practice! Practice your predetermined small talk topics in the mirror before social engagements.
- **Step 3**: Ask open-ended questions to keep the conversation going.
- **Step 4**: Don't force the conversion to stay on track. Let it wander and enjoy the ride.
- **Step 5**: Remember that body language is as important as words.

While small talk may seem trivial, it plays a crucial role in establishing rapport and forging a connection with others. Through active listening, asking open-ended questions, and sharing personal stories in a tactful manner, we can cultivate interpersonal relationships that go beyond mere acquaintance to true friendship. Whether we're networking at a professional event or chatting with acquaintances at a social gathering, mastering the art of small talk can open countless doors and lead to a more fulfilling and well-rounded life. Remember, small talk need not be superficial or insincere, but can be a powerful tool for crafting authentic connections with those around us.

A CHANCE TO HELP SOMEONE ELSE

Slowly but surely, you'll find that social situations get easier as you employ these techniques and strategies... and this is your chance to help someone else reap the same benefits.

Simply by sharing your honest opinion of this book and a little about your own experience, you'll show new readers where they can find the help they're longing for.

WANT TO HELP OTHERS?

Thank you for your support. You may never meet them, but someone out there will thank you for it.

Scan the QR code to leave your review on Amazon.

CONCLUSION

It's important to acknowledge that navigating social interactions can be challenging for those who feel socially awkward. Engaging with new people can evoke discomfort and uncertainty. However, effective communication is the key to unlocking a world of possibilities and personal growth.

You realize that successful communication is essential for achieving your goals and creating meaningful connections. It requires stepping out of your comfort zone and making some adjustments along the way. Embracing discomfort is necessary for transformative change. Let go of pessimism and embrace optimism, nurturing a positive outlook that bolsters your self-confidence.

Understanding the unique challenges that contribute to your social awkwardness is crucial. By gaining insights into your specific struggles, you can develop personalized strategies to navigate social interactions with greater ease and authenticity.

Remember, effective communication extends beyond mere words. Pay attention to nonverbal cues, master active listening, and ask thoughtful questions to foster engaging conversations. As you practice these skills, small talk will become more natural and effortless.

By embracing the strategies, ideas, and tips shared in this book and putting them into practice, you'll gradually become a skilled communicator who can connect with anyone, regardless of the situation.

I have unwavering faith in your ability to achieve your communication goals. With time and dedication, you will find yourself engaging in conversations without succumbing to self-doubt, negativity, or isolation. Embrace your unique strengths, seize the opportunities that come your way, and confidently navigate the vast landscape of social interactions.

You possess the potential to make a lasting impact, so go forth, wear a smile, and embrace your role in shaping the world around you.

REFERENCES

13 Ways to communicate with confidence. (2023, February 6). Understanding ModernGov. https://blog.moderngov.com/how-to-communicate-with-confidence

13 Ways to overcome negative thought patterns. (2016, May 9). *13 Ways to overcome negative thought patterns. Forbes.* https://www.forbes.com/sites/forbescoachescouncil/2016/05/09/13-coaches-explain-how-to-overcome-negative-thought-patterns/?sh=311020ef35cb

40 potent quotes that remind us of the power of conversation. (2022, July 26). BestSelf Co. https://bestself.co/blogs/the-bestself-hub/40-potent-quotes-that-remind-us-of-the-power-of-conversation

Active listening. (n.d). Skills You Need. https://www.skillsyouneed.com/ips/active-listening.html

Arzt, N. (2023, January 26). *Shyness vs. social anxiety: Understanding the difference.* Choosing Therapy. https://www.choosingtherapy.com/social-anxiety-vs-shyness/

Amati, V., Meggiolaro, S., Rivellini, G., & Zaccarin, S. (2018). Social relations and life satisfaction: the role of friends. *Genus, 74*(1). https://doi.org/10.1186/s41118-018-0032-z

Ayanthi. (n.d). *Communicating with difficult people: A how-to guide.* The Indigo Project.https://www.theindigoproject.com.au/communicating-with-difficult-people-a-how-to-guide/

Brooks, A., & John, L. (2018, May). The surprising power of questions. *Harvard Business Review.* https://hbr.org/2018/05/the-surprising-power-of-questions

Cherry, K. (2022, February 24). *Why You May Not Know How to Connect With People.* Very Well Mind. https://www.verywellmind.com/i-cant-connect-with-people-why-you-might-feel-this-way-5219583#toc-factors-that-make-it-difficult-to-connect-with-people

Cherry, K. (2022, November 29). *Phineas Gage: His accident and impact on society.* Very Well Mind. https://www.verywellmind.com/ phineas-gage-2795244#toc-phineas-gages-impact-on-psychology

Cherry, K. (2022, November 14). *What is the negativity basis?* Very Well Mind. https://www.verywellmind.com/negative-bias-4589618

Cherry, K. (2023, February 22). *Types of nonverbal communication.* Very Well Mind. https://www.verywellmind.com/types-of-nonverbal-communication-2795397

Cooks-Campbell, A. (2022, April 28). *How to deal with difficult people—without harming your health.* Better Up. https://www.betterup.com/ blog/how-to-deal-with-difficult-people

Cuncic, A. (2023, February 15). *Small talk topics.* Very Well Mind. https://www.verywellmind.com/small-talk-topics-3024421#toc-frequently-asked-questions-188f61f3-c382-433d-baff-330b35f1dfcc

Darcy, A. M. (2023, March 3). *Emotional awareness— What it is and why you need it.* Harley Therapy. https://www.harleytherapy.co.uk/coun selling/emotional-awareness.htm

Fletcher, J. (2015, June 30). *The important connection between body language and EQ.* Linkedin.https://www.linkedin.com/pulse/impor tant-connection-between-body-language-eq-joan-fletcher/

Frost, A. (2019, July 24). *The ultimate guide to small talk: Conversation starters, powerful questions & more.* Hubspot. https://blog.hubspot. com/sales/small-talk-guide

Geikham, Y. (2022, July 20). *Be social: 7 English small talk topics for starting friendly conversations.* Fluentu. https://www.fluentu.com/ blog/english/english-small-talk/

Gill, M. (2021, April 22). *The science behind social anxiety.* Healing Holidays. https://www.healingholidays.com/blog/the-science-behind-social-anxiety

Graebner, K. (2021, June 18). *How to practice self-compassion and tame your inner critic.* Better Up. https://www.betterup.com/blog/self-compassion

Granneman, J. (2019, August 15). *The science behind why introverts struggle to put their thoughts into words.* Introvert, Dear. https://intro

vertdear.com/news/the-science-behind-why-introverts-struggle-to-speak/

Hardcastle, F. (2021, August 19). *How to become a confident communicator.* Baltic Apprenticeships. https://www.balticapprenticeships.com/blog/how-to-become-a-confident-communicator

How does negative thinking affect your social skills? (n.d). The Social Skills Centre. https://socialskillscenter.com/how-does-negative-thinking-affect-your-social-skills/?utm_source=rss&utm_medium=rss&utm_campaign=how-does-negative-thinking-affect-your-social-skills

How to build self-confidence. (n.d). Reach Out. https://au.reachout.com/articles/how-to-build-self-confidence

Hulis, A. (2023, February 10). *5 Ways a lack of communication can impact your career.* Fairy God Boss. https://fairygodboss.com/articles/lack-of-communication

Lapum, J. (2020). *Introduction to communication in nursing.* https://pressbooks.library.torontomu.ca/communicationnursing/chapter/communication-is-learned/

Lomanowska, A. M., & Guitton, M. J. (2016). Online intimacy and well-being in the digital age. *Internet Interventions, 4,* 138–144. https://doi.org/10.1016/j.invent.2016.06.005

Luke – confidence and communication skills flourish together. (2018, August 22). Interactionz. https://www.interactionz.org.nz/blog/post/31716/Luke--confidence-and-communication-skills-flourish-together/

Mack, S. (2020, April 11). *How confidence affects communication, what to avoid and how to improve yours.* ExcellenceXL. https://excellencexl.com/how-confidence-affects-communication-how-to-improve/

Martins, J. (2022, October 27). *Listening to understand: How to practice active listening (with examples).* Asana. https://asana.com/resources/active-listening

Matejko, S. (2022, October 11). *Social awkwardness: Signs and how to overcome it.* PsychCentral. https://psychcentral.com/health/socially-awkward

Mertz, J. (2012, September 24). *The importance of questions in conversa-*

tion. Thin Difference. https://www.thindifference.com/2012/09/the-importance-of-questions-in-conversations/

Moore, C. (2019, June 2). *How to practice self-compassion: 8 Techniques and tips*. Positive Psychology. https://positivepsychology.com/how-to-practice-self-compassion/#show-self-compassion

Moore, M. (2022, February 25). *How a lack of clear communication can affect your life, and ways to improve it*. PsychCentral. https://psychcentral.com/blog/is-lack-of-communication-a-red-flag

O'Bryan. A. (2022, February 8). *How to practice active listening: 16 Examples & techniques*. Positive Psychology. https://positivepsychology.com/active-listening-techniques/#techniques

Perera, K. (n.d). *How does self-esteem affect communication skills?* More Self-Esteem. https://more-selfesteem.com/how-does-self-esteem-affect-communication-skills/

Perry, E. (2023, January 30). *Learn how to ask good questions to keep the conversation going*. Better Up. https://www.betterup.com/blog/how-to-ask-good-questions#one

Schultz, J. (2021, July 8). *Reasons to keep asking questions*. Linkedin. https://www.linkedin.com/pulse/reasons-keep-asking-questions-jonathan-schultz/

Segal et al. (2023, March 1). *Nonverbal communication and body language*. HelpGuide.org. https://www.helpguide.org/articles/relationships-communication/nonverbal-communication.htm

Self-esteem. (n.d.). Grand Rapids Counseling Services. https://grcounseling.com/self-esteem/

Serin et al. (2012). The relationships among negative thoughts, problem solving and social skills of school psychological consultants. *Eurasian Journal of Educational Research. 12*(49A), 67-82. https://www.researchgate.net/publication/298416406_The_Relationships_Among_Negative_Thoughts_Problem_Solving_and_Social_Skills_of_School_Psychological_Consultants

Social awkward: Symptoms and facts. (2018, March 5). King University Online. https://online.king.edu/news/socially-awkward-symptoms/

Social Anxiety Disorder. (n.d.). National Institute of Mental Health (NIMH). https://www.nimh.nih.gov/health/statistics/social-anxiety-disorder

Stolk, A. (2017, May 8). *Human communication and the brain. Frontiers.* https://kids.frontiersin.org/articles/10.3389/frym.2017.00012

Tips for communicating with difficult people. (2018, August 13). Biltmore Psychology and Counseling. https://www.biltmorecounseling.com/biltmore/tips-for-communicating-with-difficult-people/

Valcour, M. (2017, May 22). *8 Ways to get a difficult conversation back on track. Harvard Business Review.* https://hbr.org/2017/05/8-ways-to-get-a-difficult-conversation-back-on-track

Van Edwards, V. (n.d). *How to have and hold dazzling conversations with anyone: We review 11 science backed steps.* Science of People. https://www.scienceofpeople.com/have-hold-conversation/

Van Edwards, V. (n.d). *How to read people and decode 7 body language cues.* Science of People. https://www.scienceofpeople.com/how-to-read-people/

Van Edwards, V. (n.d). *4 Types of difficult people and how to deal with them.* Science of People. https://www.scienceofpeople.com/difficult-people/

What is active listening? 4 Tips for improving communication skills. (2021, March 10). Colorado State University Global. https://csuglobal.edu/blog/what-active-listening-4-tips-improving-communication-skills

Why is language important? Your guide to spoken word. (n.d). University of the People. https://www.uopeople.edu/blog/why-is-language-important/

Ye, L. (2017, June 22). *5 Psychology-backed exercises that will make you feel more confident.* Hubspot. https://blog.hubspot.com/sales/psychology-backed-exercises-more-confident

Made in the USA
Las Vegas, NV
06 January 2024

83988083R00109